NEW SCIENCE LIBRARY

presents traditional topics from a modern perspective, particularly those associated with the hard sciences—physics,
biology, and medicine—and those of the human sciences—
psychology, sociology, and philosophy.

The aim of this series is the enrichment of both the scientific and spiritual view of the world through their mutual
dialogue and exchange.

New Science Library is an imprint of Shambhala Publications.

General Editor   Ken Wilber
Consulting Editors Jeremy W. Hayward
                   Francisco Varela

THE TREE OF KNOWLEDGE

The Biological Roots of Human Understanding

Humberto R. Maturana & Francisco J. Varela

Translated by Robert Paolucci

FOREWORD BY J. Z. YOUNG

NEW SCIENCE LIBRARY
Shambhala
Boston & London
1988

NEW SCIENCE LIBRARY
An imprint of
Shambhala Publications, Inc.
Horticultural Hall
300 Massachusetts Avenue
Boston, Massachusetts 02115

9 8 7 6 5 4 3 2 1

FIRST PAPERBACK EDITION
Printed in the United States of America

Distributed in the United States by Random House
and in Canada by Random House of Canada Ltd.

The Library of Congress Catalogues the hardcover
edition of this work as follows:

Maturana, Humberto R., 1928–
   The tree of knowledge.
   Translation of: El árbol del conocimiento.
   Includes index.
   1. Cognition—Physiological aspects.
2. Learning—Physiological aspects.   3. Neuropsychology.
I. Varela, Francisco J., 1946– .   II. Title.
QP395.M3813   1987   612'.8   86-29698
ISBN 0-87773-373-2
ISBN 0-87773-403-8 (pbk.)

COVER ART: *The Three Sphinxes of Bikini* (1947) by Salvador Dali. Oil on canvas, 30 × 50 cm, Galerie Petit, Paris. Copyright Demart Pro Arte B.V./Salvador Dali. Photograph by Robert Descharnes. Reproduced with permission.

Contents

Foreword

This book will start readers thinking in new ways
about both science and philosophy. The authors
have been most ingenious in finding means to explain at the same our human processes of thought
and the facts of biology. There are fresh insights
on every page, presented very clearly. Dr. Maturana and Dr. Varela, well known for finding new
approaches in nerve physiology, have produced a
truly original book, which will be a revelation and
inspiration to many people.

Professor J. Z. YOUNG
Oxford University

Preface

The book that you now hold in your hands is not just another introduction to the biology of cognition. It is a complete outline for an alternative view of the biological roots of understanding. From the outset we warn readers that the view presented here will not coincide with those they are likely to be familiar with. Indeed, we will propose a way of seeing cognition not as a representation of the world "out there," but rather as an ongoing bringing forth of a world through the process of living itself.

To accomplish this goal, we shall follow a rigorous conceptual itinerary, wherein every concept builds on preceding ones, until the whole is an indissociable network. We thus discourage a casual, diagonal reading of this book. In compensation, we have done our best to provide a wealth of illustrations and a conceptual map of salient ideas, clearly indicated in the text as separate boxes, so that readers can always find where they are standing along the journey.

This book came into being as a consequence of very particular circumstances. In 1980 the Organization of American States (OAS) was actively seeking ways to understand the many difficulties confronted in social communication and knowledge transfer. Aware of this need, Rolf Benhcke, then with ODEPLAN (the Ministry of Planning of the Chilean government), immediately thought it would be beneficial to expose the OAS to our approach to those issues, in the form of a coherent formulation of the foundations of communication as the biological being of man. The OAS accepted the idea, and a contract was signed. The project began in September 1980 with a series of lectures delivered to an audience of mostly social workers and managers, given alternately by both authors. These lectures were transcribed, extensively edited during 1981–1983, and published as a book printed privately in 1985 for the internal distribution of OAS. Excepting some minor corrections and additions, that initial text is the present book. Thus, we are very grateful to the OAS for its interest and financial support and for giving us the freedom to publish the text independently. Most particularly we are indebted to Mr. Benhcke, who put heart and soul into seeing this project come to fruition. Finally, Francisco Olivares and his associates, who labored for months over the many illustrations of this book, should be acknowledged with many thanks for their excellent performance. Without the concurrence of each and all of these persons and institutions, this book would not have been possible.

A word about the history of the ideas contained in this book is also in order. They can be traced back to 1960, when Humberto Maturana began to depart from habitual biological tradition and tried to conceive of living systems in terms of the processes that realized them, and not in terms of the relationship with an environment. That exploration continued over the next decade and attained a first clear manifestation in his article "The Neurophysiology of Cognition,"[1] published in 1969, in which some of the key ideas on the circular organization of living system were expounded. Fran-

1. H. R. Maturana, "The Neurophysiology of Cognition," in P. Garvin, *Cognition: A Multiple View* (New York: Spartan Books, 1969). The final version of this paper appeared as H. R. Maturana, "The Biology of Cognition," BCL Report no. 9.0, 1970, reprinted in *Autopoiesis and Cognition* (see footnote 3).

cisco Varela had started as Maturana's student in the mid-1960s, and by 1970, the two of us, now working as colleagues at the University of Chile, continued on the trail to produce a reformulation of the biological phenomenology in a small book entitled *Autopoiesis: The Organization of the Living*, written during 1970–1971 and first published in 1973.[2] Both these "foundational" papers are now available in the book *Autopoiesis and Cognition*.[3] The political events in Chile in 1973 led both of us to continue our research in distant places and in our own styles, covering new theoretical and experimental ground.[4] Much later, in 1980, when circumstances again made it possible, our collaboration was resumed in Santiago. The present book incorporates ideas developed independently or jointly by both of us during all these years. It represents in our eyes a fresh, accessible synthesis of a view of life and mind that we have come to share, starting from the early intuitions of Maturana more than twenty-five years before.

More than anything, this text is an invitation for readers to let go of their usual certainties and thus to come into a different biological insight of what it is to be human.

2. H. R. Maturana and F. J. Varela, *De máquinas y seres vivos: Una teoría de la organización biológica* (Santiago, Editorial Universitaria, 1973). English version in *Autopoiesis and Cognition* (see footnote 3).

3. H. Maturana and F. Varela, *Autopoiesis and Cognition: The Realization of the Living* (Boston: D. Reidel, 1980).

4. See, for example, H. R. Maturana, "Biology of Language: Epistemology of Reality," in *Psychology and Biology of Language and Thought*, ed. G. Miller and E. Lenneberg (New York: Academic Press, 1978); F. J. Varela, *Principles of Biological Autonomy* (New York: North-Holland, 1979).

The Tree of Knowledge

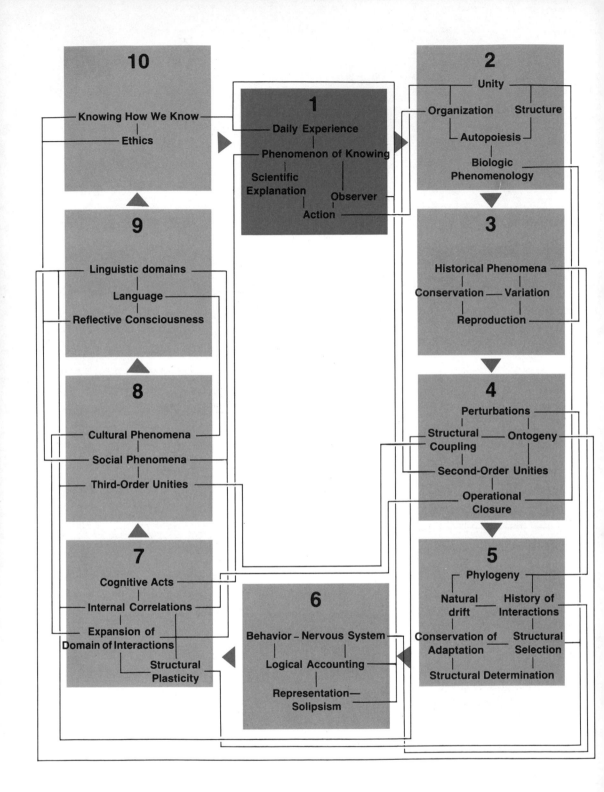

10

Knowing How We Know

Ethics

1

Daily Experience

Phenomenon of Knowing

Scientific
Explanation

Observer

Action

2

Unity

Organization   Structure

Autopoiesis

Biologic
Phenomenology

9

Linguistic domains

Language

Reflective Consciousness

3

Historical Phenomena

Conservation — Variation

Reproduction

8

Cultural Phenomena

Social Phenomena

Third-Order Unities

4

Perturbations

Structural   Ontogeny
Coupling

Second-Order Unities

Operational
Closure

7

Cognitive Acts

Internal Correlations

Expansion of
Domain of Interactions

Structural
Plasticity

6

Behavior – Nervous System

Logical Accounting

Representation—
Solipsism

5

Phylogeny

Natural   History of
drift   Interactions

Conservation of   Structural
Adaptation   Selection

Structural Determination

Knowing How We Know

The Great Temptation

In Figure 1 we admire *Christ Crowned with Thorns* by the master from 's-Hertogenbosch, better known as Bosch. This untraditional portrayal of the crowning with thorns depicts the scene almost in a flat plane, with large heads. More than a single incident in the Passion, it suggests a universal sense of evil contrasted with the kingdom of heaven. Christ, in the center, expresses the utmost patience and acceptance. His tormentors, however, were not painted here, as in so many other works in the time and by Bosch himself, with otherworldly figures directly attacking Christ, pulling his hair or piercing his flesh. The attackers appear as four human types that in the medieval mind represented a total view of humanity. Each one of these types is like a great temptation against the expansiveness and patience of Christ's expression. They are four styles of estrangement and loss of interior calm.

There is much to meditate on and contemplate about in these four temptations. For us who are beginning the long journey of this book, however, the figure at the lower right is particularly relevant. He is grabbing Jesus by the robe, tugging him to the ground. He holds on to him and restricts his freedom, fastening his attention on him. He seems to be telling him: "Now listen to

Fig. 1. *Christ Crowned with Thorns* by Hieronymus Bosch, National Museum of the Prado, Madrid.

me, I know what I'm saying!" This is the temptation of *certainty*.

We tend to live in a world of certainty, of undoubted, rock-ribbed perceptions: our convictions prove that things are the way we see them and there is no alternative to what we hold as true. This is our daily situation, our cultural condition, our common way of being human.

Now, this whole book is a sort of invitation to refrain from the habit of falling into the temptation of certainty. This is necessary for two reasons. On the one hand, if the reader does not suspend his certainties, we cannot communicate anything here that will be embodied in his experience as an effective understanding of the phenomenon of cognition. On the other hand, what this book aims to show, by scrutinizing the phenomenon of cognition and our actions flowing from it, is that all cognitive experience involves the knower in a personal way, rooted in his biological structure. There, his experience of certainty is an individual phenomenon blind to the cognitive acts of others, in a solitude which, as we shall see, is transcended only in a world created with those others.

Surprises of the Eye

Nothing we are going to say will be understood in a really effective way unless the reader feels personally involved and has a direct experience that goes beyond all mere description.

So, instead of telling why the apparent firmness of our experiential world suddenly wavers when we look at it up close, we shall demonstrate this with two single examples. Both correspond to the sphere of our daily visual experience.

First example: Cover your left eye and stare at the cross in Figure 2. Hold the page about fifteen inches away from you. You'll notice the black dot in the drawing, not small in size, suddenly disappear. Experiment by rotating the page a bit or opening your other eye. It is also interesting to copy the drawing on another sheet of paper and gradually enlarge the black dot until it reaches the maximum size at which it disappears. Further, rotate the page so that point B is in the place where point A was, and repeat the observation. What happened to the line that crosses the dot?

Actually, this same situation can be observed without any drawing: simply replace the cross on the dot with your thumb. The thumb looks as if it is cut off. (Try it!) Incidentally, this is how the observation became popular: Marriot, a scientist at the French court, showed King Louis by this process how his subjects would look beheaded before he had their heads cut off.

The commonly accepted explanation of this phenomenon is that the image of the dot (or the thumb or the subject), in that specific position, falls into the area of the retina where the optic nerve emerges; hence, it is not sensitive to light. It is called the blind spot. What is rarely stressed in giving this explanation, however, is: How come we don't go around with a hole that size all the time? Our visual experience is of a continuous space. Unless we do these ingenious manipulations, we will not perceive the discontinuity that is always there. The fascinating thing about the experiment with the blind spot is that *we do not see that we do not see.*

Second example: Let us take two sources of light and place them as in Figure 4. (This can be done by making a hard paper tube the size of a strong

Fig. 2. Experiment of the blind spot.

A

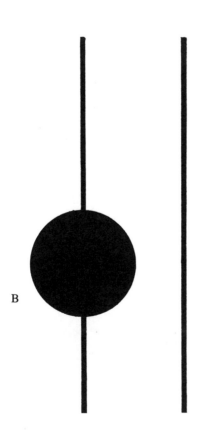

B

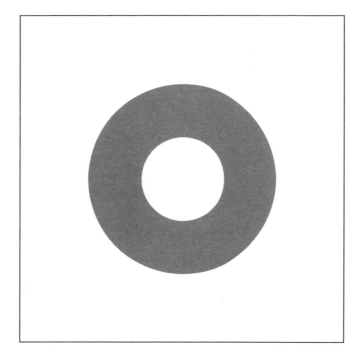

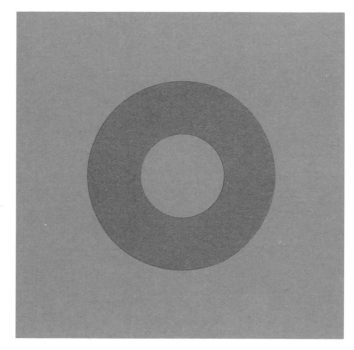

Fig. 3. The two circles on this page were printed with identical ink. The one below, however, appears rose-colored because of the green around it. Moral: Color is not a property of things; it is inseparable from the way we see it.

Fig. 4. Colored shadows.

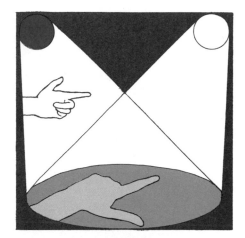

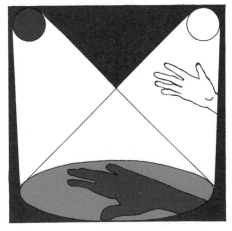

light bulb and using some red cellophane as a filter.) Then place an object, such as your hand, in the beam of light. Note the shadows on the wall. One of the shadows looks bluish-green in color! The reader can experiment by using different-colored transparent papers in front of the lights and different light intensities.

The example here is as surprising as in the case of the blind spot. Why do we get a bluish-green color when we simply expected white, red, and mixtures of white with red (pink)? We are used to thinking that color is a quality of objects and of the light they reflect. Thus, if I see green, it must be because a green light is reaching my eye, that is, light of a certain wavelength. Now, if we take an instrument to measure the light composition in this example, we find that there is no predominance of wavelengths called green or blue in the shadow we see as bluish-green, but only the distribution proper to white light. Our experience of greenish-blue, however, is something we cannot deny.

This beautiful phenomenon of the so-called colored shadows was first described by Otto von Guericke in 1672. He noted that his finger appeared blue in the shadow between the light from his candle and the rising sun. Confronted with this and similar phenomena, people usually say: "Fine, but what color is it *really?*—as though the answer given by the instrument that measures wavelengths were the ultimate answer. Actually, this simple experiment does not reveal an isolated situation that could be called (as is often the case) marginal or illusory. Our experience with a world of colored objects is literally independent of the wavelength composition of the light coming from any scene we look at. In point of fact, if I take an

orange from my room to the patio, the orange still
seems to be of the same color; however, the inside
of the house was illumined by flourescent light,
which has a great number of so-called blue (or
short) wavelengths, whereas the sun has mostly
so-called red (or long) wavelengths. There is no
way we can trace a correspondence between the
great color consistency of the objects we see and
the light that comes from them. It is not easy to
explain how we see colors, and we shall not try
to do so here in detail. But the important thing, to
explain it, is for us to stop thinking that the color
of the objects we see is determined by the features of the light we receive from the objects.
Rather, we must concentrate on understanding
that the experience of a color corresponds to a
specific pattern of states of activity in the nervous
system which its structure determines. In fact,
although we shall not do it right now, we can
demonstrate that because these states of neuronal
activity (as when we see green) can be triggered
by a number of different light perturbations (like
those which make it possible to see colored shadows), we can correlate our naming of colors with
states of neuronal activity but not with wavelengths. What states of neuronal activity are triggered by the different perturbations is determined
in each person by his or her individual structure
and not by the features of the perturbing agent.

The foregoing is valid for all the dimensions of
visual experience (movement, texture, form, etc.),
as also for any other perceptual modality. We could
give similar examples that show us, at one stroke,
that what we took as a simple apprehension of
something (such as space or color) has the indel-
ible mark of our own structure. We shall have to
content ourselves for now with the observations

given. We trust that the reader has tested them. Therefore, we assume that the reliability of his or her experience has been shaken.

These experiences—and many others like them—contain in a nutshell the essential flavor of what we wish to say. That is, they show how our experience is moored to our structure in a binding way. We do not see the "space" of the world; we live our field of vision. We do not see the "colors" of the world; we live our chromatic space. Doubtless, as we shall note throughout these pages, we are experiencing a world. But when we examine more closely how we get to know this world, we invariably find that we cannot separate our history of actions—biological and social—from how this world appears to us. It is so obvious and close that it is very hard to see.

A Crying Shame

In the Bronx Zoo in New York City there is a special pavilion for primates. There we can see chimpanzees, gorillas, and many monkeys of the Old and New Worlds. Our attention is drawn, however, to a separate cage at the back of the pavilion. It is enclosed with thick bars and bears a sign that says: "The Most Dangerous Primate in the World." As we look between the bars, we see with surprise our own face; the caption explains that man has destroyed more species on the earth than any other animal known. From being observers we go on to be the observed (by ourselves). But what do we see?

The moment of reflection before a mirror is always a peculiar moment: it is the moment when we become aware of that part of ourselves which we cannot see in any other way—as when we re-

veal the blind spot that shows us our own structure; as when we suppress the blindness that it
entails, filling the blank space. Reflection is a process of knowing how we know. It is an act of turn-
ing back upon ourselves. It is the only chance we
have to discover our blindness and to recognize
that the certainties and knowledge of others are,
respectively, as overwhelming and tenuous as
our own.

This special situation of knowing how we know
is traditionally elusive for our Western culture. We
are keyed to action and not to reflection, so that
our personal life is generally blind to itself. It is as
though a taboo tells us: "It is forbidden to know
about knowing." Actually, not knowing what
makes up our world of experience, which is the
closest world to us, is a crying shame. There are
many things to be ashamed about in the world,
but this ignorance is one of the worst.

Maybe one of the reasons why we avoid tapping
the roots of our knowledge is that it gives us a
slightly dizzy sensation due to the circularity entailed in using the instrument of analysis to analyze the instrument of analysis. It is like asking an
eye to see itself. Figure 5, a drawing by the Dutch
artist M. C. Escher, shows this dizziness very
clearly: hands are drawing each other in such a
way that the origin of the process is unknown:
Which is the "real" hand?

Likewise, although we saw that the processes
involved in our activities, in our makeup, in our
actions as human beings, constitute our knowledge, we intend to investigate how we know, by
looking at these things by means of those processes. We have no alternative, however, because
what we do is inseparable from our experience of
the world with all its regularities: its commercial

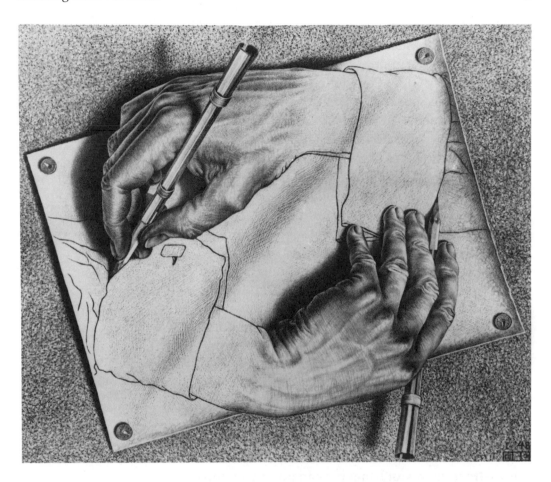

Fig. 5. *Drawing Hands* by M. C. Escher.

centers, its children, its atomic wars. What we do intend—and the reader should make it a personal task—is to be aware of what is implied in this unbroken coincidence of our being, our doing, and our knowing. We shall put aside our daily tendency to treat our experience with the seal of certainty, as though it reflected an absolute world.

Therefore, underlying everything we shall say is this constant awareness that the phenomenon of knowing cannot be taken as though there were "facts" or objects out there that we grasp and store in our head. The experience of anything out there is validated in a special way by the human structure, which makes possible "the thing" that arises in the description.

This circularity, this connection between action and experience, this inseparability between a particular way of being and how the world appears to us, tells us that *every act of knowing brings forth a world*. This feature of knowing will invariably be our problem, our starting point, and the guideline of all that we present in the following pages. All this can be summed up in the aphorism *All doing is knowing, and all knowing is doing*.

When we speak here of action and experience, we mean something different from what occurs only in relation to the surrounding world, on the purely "physical" level. This feature of human activity applies to all the dimensions of our daily life. In particular, it applies to what we—the reader and the writer—are doing right here and now. And what are we doing? We are dealing in language, breezing along in a distinctive way of conversing in an imagined dialogue. Every reflection, including one on the foundation of human knowledge, invariably takes place in language, which is our distinctive way of being human and being humanly active. For this reason, language is also our starting point, our cognitive instrument, and our sticking point. It is very important not to forget that circularity between action and experience applies also to what we are doing here and now. To do so would have serious consequences, as the reader will see further on. At no time should we forget this. And to this end, we shall sum it all up in a second aphorism that we should keep in mind throughout this book: *Everything said is said by someone*. Every reflection brings forth a world. As

Key Sayings

"All doing is knowing and
all knowing is doing."

"Everything said is said by someone."

such, it is a human action by someone in particular in a particular place.

These two aphorisms ought to be like two guiding lights that permanently remind us where we came from and where we are going.

This bringing forth of knowledge is commonly regarded as a stumbling block, an error or an explanatory residue to be eradicated. This is why, for instance, a colored shadow is said to be an "optical illusion" and why "in reality" there is no color. What we are saying is exactly the opposite: this characteristic of knowledge is the master key to understanding it, not an annoying residue or obstacle. Bringing forth a world is the burning issue of knowledge. It is associated with the deepest roots of our cognitive being, however strong our experience may be. And because these roots go to the very biologic base—as we shall see—this bringing forth of a world manifests itself in *all* our actions and all our being. Certainly, it manifests itself in all those actions of human social life where it is often evident, as in the case of values and preferences. But there is no discontinuity between what is social and what is human and their biological roots. The phenomenon of knowing is all of one piece, and in its full scope it has one same groundwork.

Our objective is then clear; we wish to examine the phenomenon of cognition by considering the universal nature of "doing" in cognition—this bringing forth of a world—as our problem and starting point, so as to show its foundation. And what will be our yardstick for saying that we have been successful in our attempt? An explanation is always a proposition that reformulates or re-creates the observations of a phenomenon in a system of concepts acceptable to a group of people who share a criterion of validation. Magic, for instance, is as explanatory for those who accept it as science is for those who accept it. The specific difference between a magical explanation and a scientific one lies in the way a system of scientific explanations is made, what constitutes its criterion of validation. Thus, we can distinguish four conditions essential to proposing a scientific explanation. They do not necessarily fall in sequential order but do overlap in some way. They are:

Explanation

a. Describing the phenomenon (or phenomena) to be explained in a way acceptable to a body of observers

b. Proposing a conceptual system capable of generating the phenomenon to be explained in a way acceptable to a body of observers (explanatory hypothesis)

c. Obtaining from (b) other phenomena not explicitly considered in that proposition, as also describing its conditions for observation by a body of observers

d. Observing these other phenomena obtained from (b).

Only when this criterion of validation is satisfied will the explanation be a scientific one, and a

Explaining Cognition

I. Phenomenon to be explained: the effective action of a living being in its environment

II. Explanatory hypothesis: autonomous organization of living beings; phylogenetic and ontogenetic drift with conservation of adaptation (structural coupling)

III. Obtaining other phenomena: behavioral coordination in interactions recurring between living beings and recursive behavioral coordination upon behavioral coordination

IV. Further observations: social phenomena, linguistic domains, language, and self-consciousness

Knowing

Knowing is effective action, that is, operating effectively in the domain of existence of living beings.

statement is a scientific one only when it is based on scientific explanations.

This four-component cycle is not alien to our daily thinking. We often use it to explain phenomena as varied as the breakdown of an automobile or the election of a president. What scientists do is try to be wholly consistent and explicit with each one of the steps. They will keep a record so as to create a tradition that will go beyond one person or one generation.

Our situation is exactly the same. We, the readers and the writers, have become observers who make descriptions. As observers, we have focused on cognition as our phenomenon to be explained. Moreover, what we have said points to our starting description of the phenomenon of cognition. Since all cognition brings forth a world, our starting point will necessarily be the operational effectiveness of living beings in their domain of existence. In other words, our starting point to get an explanation that can be scientifically validated is to characterize cognition as an *effective action*, an

action that will enable a living being to continue
its existence in a definite environment as it brings
forth its world. Nothing more, nothing less.

And how can we tell when we have reached a
satisfactory explanation of the phenomenon of
knowing? Well, by now the reader can guess the
answer: when we have set forth a conceptual system that can *generate* the cognitive phenomenon
as a result of the action of a living being, and
when we have shown that this process can produce living beings like ourselves, able to generate
descriptions and reflect on them as a result of
their fulfillment as living beings operating effectively in their fields of existence. From this explanatory proposition we shall have to see just
how all our familiar dimensions of knowing are
generated.

This is the odyssey we set for the reader in these
pages. Throughout the chapters that follow, we
shall be developing both this explanatory proposition and its connection to additional phenomena
such as communication and language. At the end
of this journey, the reader can go over these pages
again and assess how fruitful it was to accept our
invitation to look thus at the phenomenon of
knowing.

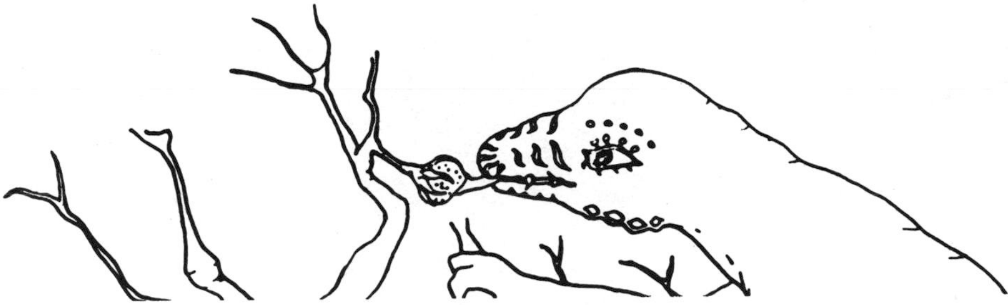

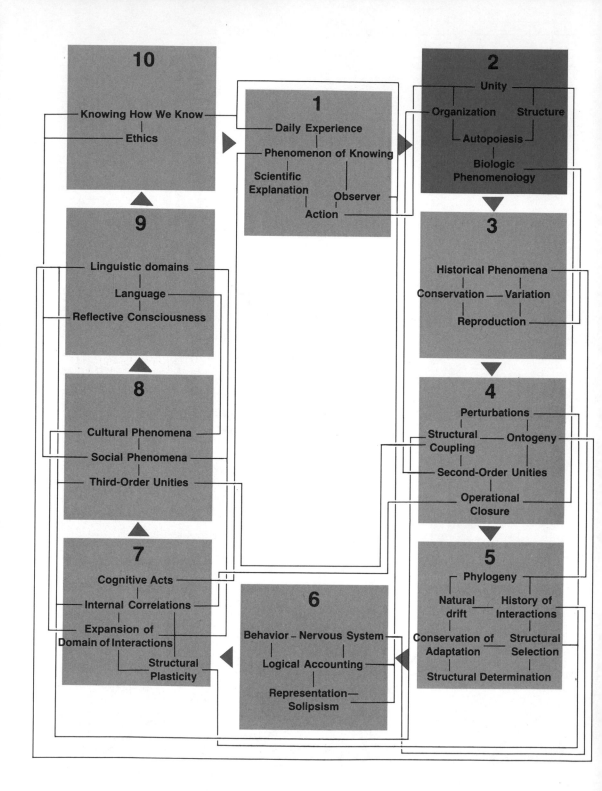

2   The Organization of Living Things

Fig. 6. Spiral nebula NGC 1566
in the Dorado constellation.

Our starting point has been the awareness that all knowing is an action by the knower, that is, that all knowing depends on the structure of the knower. And this starting point will be the signpost to our conceptual journey throughout these pages: how is knowledge brought forth in "doing"? What are the roots and mechanisms that make it operate in this way?

In the light of these questions, the first step along our journey is as follows: knowing is the action of the knower; it is rooted in the very manner of his *living being*, in his *organization*. We hold that the biological roots of knowing cannot be understood only through examining the nervous system; we believe it is necessary to understand how these processes are rooted in the living being as a whole.

Therefore, in this chapter we are going to discuss a few things about the organization of living things. This discussion will not be an ornament of biology or a kind of crash course for those who lack biological training. In this book it is a key feature to help us understand the phenomenon of cognition in all its facets.

A Brief History of the Earth

To take our first steps toward understanding the organization of living beings, we shall see first how its *materiality* can serve as a guide to its keystone. On our trip let us travel by some landmarks of material transformation that make it possible for living beings to *appear*.

Figure 6 shows the so-called galaxy NGC 1566 of the Dorado Constellation. It is commonly known as the Austral Galaxy, a very bright spiral galaxy. Not only is it beautiful but it is especially

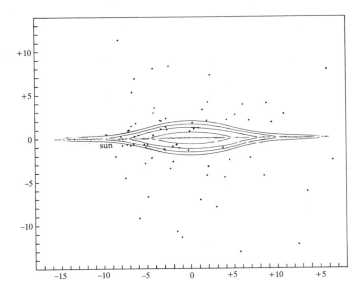

Fig. 7. Distances in the Milky Way and the location of our sun in it.

interesting to us because our own galaxy, the Milky Way, would appear very similar in shape if seen from afar. Failing that, we must content ourselves with a diagram such as that in Figure 7. It shows some dimensions of stellar space and stars that, compared with our own, make us feel very humble. The scale units are in kiloparsecs, and each one of them is 3,260 light-years. Within the Milky Way, our solar system has a rather peripheral position of about 8 kiloparsecs from the center.

Our sun is one of so many million other stars that make up these multifaceted structures called galaxies. How did these stars originate? The following reconstruction of their history has been proposed.

Interstellar space contains enormous amounts of hydrogen. Turbulence in these gaseous masses causes high-density gas pockets, shown in the first stages of Figure 8. In this state, something very interesting begins to happen: an equilibrium takes place between the tendency to cohesion due to gravity and the tendency to radiation due to

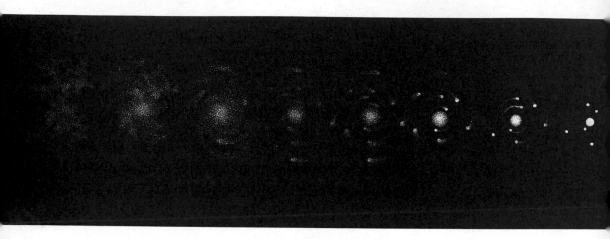

thermonuclear reactions inside the former star. This radiation, visible from the outside, enables us to see the stars as we see them in the sky, even at great distances. When both processes are in equilibrium, the star enters its so-called main sequence (Fig. 8), that is, its life course as an individual star. During this period, the matter that has been condensed is gradually consumed in thermonuclear reactions over a period of about 8 billion years. When a portion of the condensed hydrogen is consumed, the main sequence ends in a process of more dramatic transformations. First the star turns into a red giant, then into a pulsating star; lastly it transforms into a supernova and explodes in a cosmic sneeze, which causes heavy elements to form. The matter that remains in the center of the star collapses into a smaller star of very high density called a white dwarf.

Our sun lies about midway in its main sequence, and it is expected to keep radiating for at least another 3 billion years before being consumed. Many times during this transformation of a star, a halo of matter that the star draws from interstellar space rotates around the star; this halo becomes

Fig. 8. Sketch of sequence of transformations of a star in its formation.

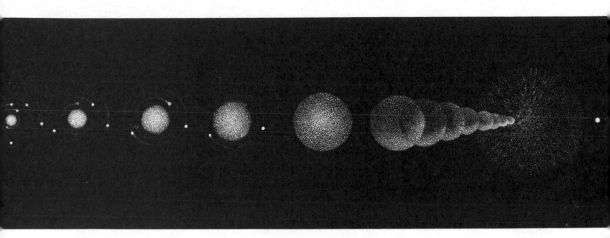

dependent on the star's course of transformations. The Earth and other planets in our planetary system are of this type. They were probably captured as remnants of a supernova explosion, for they are rich in heavyweight atoms.

According to geophysicists, the Earth is at least 5 billion years old and has a history of never-ending transformation. If we had been visitors 4 billion years ago and walked on the surface of the Earth, we would have found an atmosphere made up of gases such as methane, ammonia, hydrogen, and helium—certainly an atmosphere very different from what we know today. It would have been different because, among other things, it was constantly subject to an energy bombardment of ultraviolet radiation, gamma rays, electric discharges, meteoric impacts, and volcanic explosions. All these impacts of energy produced (and still produce) on the primitive Earth and its atmosphere an ongoing diversification of molecular species. At the dawn of star history there existed, fundamentally, molecular homogeneity. After the planets were formed, a continuous process of chemical transformation led to a great diversity of

Fig. 9. Scale comparison of
forms of (*top*) water molecules;
(*center*) an amino acid, lysine;
and (*bottom*) a protein, ribo-
nuclease enzyme.

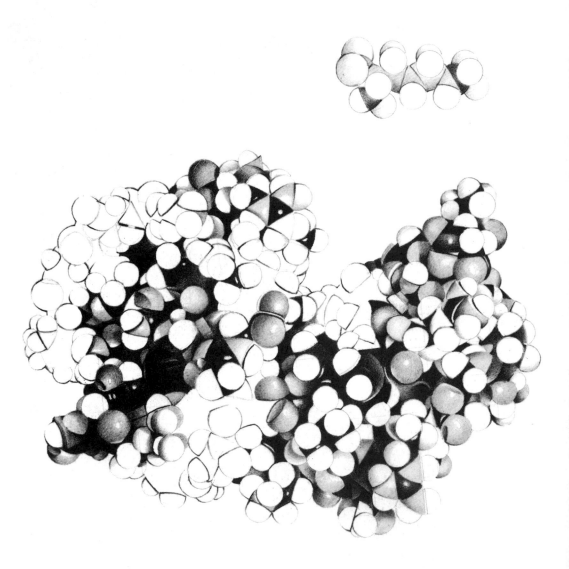

molecular species, both in the atmosphere and on the surface of the Earth.

Within this complex and continuous history of molecular transformation, however, particularly interesting to us is the moment of accumulation and diversification of the molecules formed by carbon chains, or organic molecules. Since carbon atoms can form, alone or together with many other kinds of atoms, an unlimited number of chains different in size, branching, folding, and composition, the morphologic and chemical diversity of the organic molecules is, in principle, infinite. And it is precisely this morphologic and chemical diversity of organic molecules that makes possible the existence of living beings by permitting a diversity of molecule reactions involved in the processes that produce them. We shall take this up later on. Meanwhile, let us say that anyone on primitive Earth would see the continuous abiogenic (without the participation of living beings) production of organic molecules both in the atmosphere and in the seas agitated like gigantic cauldrons of molecular reactions. Fig. 9 shows this diversity somewhat: there we see a water molecule that has only a very limited number of associations, compared with other organic molecules.

The Emergence of Living Beings

When the molecular transformations in the seas of primitive Earth reached this point, it then became possible for a particular type of molecular reaction system to form. That is to say, the potential diversification and plasticity in the family of organic molecules has made possible the formation of networks of molecular reactions that produce the same types of molecules that they embody, while at the same time they set the boundaries of the space in which they are formed. These molecular networks and interactions that produce themselves and specify their own limits are, as we shall see later, living beings.

Fig. 10 shows photographs (taken with an electron microscope) of this type of molecular grouping formed more than 3.4 billion years ago. Only a few cases of this type have been found, but they do exist. Other samples have been found in fossil deposits geologically more recent: less than 2 billion years old. Investigators have classified these molecular groupings as fossils of the first living beings—actually, as fossils of living beings still in existence today: bacteria and algae.

Distinctions

The act of indicating any being, object, thing, or unity involves making an *act of distinction* which distinguishes what has been indicated as separate from its background. Each time we refer to anything explicitly or implicitly, we are specifying a *criterion of distinction*, which indicates what we are talking about and specifies its properties as being, unity, or object.

This is a commonplace situation and not unique: we are necessarily and permanently immersed in it.

Unities

A *unity* (entity, object) is brought forth by an act of distinction. Conversely, each time we refer to a unity in our descriptions, we are implying the operation of distinction that defines it and makes it possible.

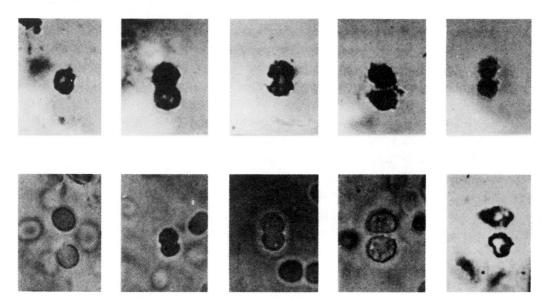

Fig. 10. *Top:* Photograph of fossils presumed to be bacteria found in deposits more than 3 billion years old. *Bottom:* Photographs of living bacteria whose form is comparable to that of the fossils.

Now, the statement "This is a fossil of a living being" is very interesting. It would be well to examine it closely. What allows an investigator to say this? Let us proceed step by step. In the first place, it was necessary to make an observation, then say there is something, some globules, whose profile can be seen under the microscope. Second, we observe that these unities thus indicated are similar, in their morphology, to living beings that exist today. As there is convincing evidence that these globules are characteristic of living beings and that these deposits date back to a time consistent with the history of transformations of the earth's surface and atmosphere associated with processes proper to living beings as we know them, the conclusion is that they are the fossils of living beings.

In point of fact, the investigator is proposing a criterion that says: living beings that existed before must resemble (in this case, morphologically) living beings today. This implies that we should have, at least implicitly, some criterion for knowing and classifying when an existing entity or system is a living being and when it is not.

This raises a sticky problem: how do I know when a being is living? What are my criteria? Throughout the history of biology many criteria have been proposed. They all have drawbacks. For instance, some have proposed as a criterion chemical composition, or the capacity to move, or reproduction, or even some combination of those criteria, that is, a list of properties. But how do we know when the list is complete? For instance, if we build a machine capable of reproducing itself, but it is made of iron and plastic and not of molecules, is it living?

We wish to give an answer to this question in a way radically different from the traditional listing of properties. This will simplify the problem tremendously. To understand this change in perspective, we have to be aware that merely asking the question of how to recognize a living being indicates that we have an idea, even if implicitly, of its *organization*. It is this idea that will determine whether we accept or reject the answer given to us. To prevent this implicit idea from entrapping and blinding us, we must be aware of it when we consider the answer that follows.

What is the makeup or organization of anything? It is both very simple and potentially complicated. "Organization" signifies those relations that must be present in order for something to exist. For me to judge that this object is a chair, I have to recognize a certain relationship between the parts I call legs, back, and seat, in such a way that sitting down is made possible. That it is made of wood and nails, or plastic and screws, has nothing at all to do with my classifying it as a chair.

This situation, in which we recognize implicitly or explicitly the organization of an object when we indicate it or distinguish it, is universal in the sense that it is something we do constantly as a basic cognitive act, which consists no more and no less than in generating classes of any type. Thus, the class of "chairs" is defined by the relations required for me to classify something as a chair. The class of "good deeds" is defined by the criteria that I establish and that must apply between the actions done and their consequences for considering them good.

It is easy to point to a certain organization by naming the objects that make up a class; however, it can be complex and hard to describe exactly and explicitly the relations that make up that organization. Thus, as regards "chairs" as a class, it may be easy to describe the organization of a "chair"; however, it is not so with the class of "good deeds," unless there is a considerable amount of cultural agreement.

When we speak of living beings, we presuppose something in common between them; otherwise we wouldn't put them in the same class we designate with the name "living." What has not been said, however, is: what is that organization that defines them as a class? Our proposition is that living beings are characterized in that, literally, they are continually self-producing. We indicate this process when we call the organization that defines them an *autopoietic organization*. Basically, this organization comes from certain relations that we shall outline and view more easily on the cellular level.

First, the molecular components of a cellular autopoietic unity must be dynamically related in a network of ongoing interactions. Today we know many of the specific chemical transformations in this network, and the biochemist collectively terms them "cell metabolism."

Now, what is distinctive about this cellular dynamics compared with any other collection of molecular transformations in natural processes? Interestingly, this cell metabolism produces components which make up the network of transformations that produced them. Some of these components form a boundary, a limit to this network of transformations. In morphologic terms, the structure that makes this cleavage in space possible is called a membrane. Now, this membranous boundary is not a product of cell metabolism in the way that fabric is the product of a

The Origin of Organic Molecules

In a discussion of the origin of organic molecules comparable to those found in living beings (such as nucleotidic bases, amino acids, or protein chains), there is often the temptation to think that there is little likelihood of their spontaneous appearance and that some guiding force is required in the entire process. From what we have outlined, this is not so. Each one of the stages described arises as an inevitable consequence of the previous one. Even today, taking a sample of the primitive atmosphere and energizing it adequately would produce organic molecules similar in complexity to those found in living beings. Even today, sufficiently compressing a gaseous hydrogen mass would produce thermonuclear reactions in it that give rise to atomic elements not present before. The history that we have been outlining is one of sequences that invariably follow one after the other, and a result would be surprising only to a person unfamiliar with the complete historical sequence.

A classic piece of evidence that there is no discontinuity in this transformation by stages was given in an experiment that Miller did in 1953 (see Fig. 11).* Miller's idea is simple: put inside a laboratory bottle an imitation of the primitive atmosphere as to composition and energy radiations. Apply an electric discharge to a mixture of ammonia, methane, hydrogen and water vapor. The results of the molecular transformations are collected by circulating water inside the bottle, and the substances that remain dissolved there are analyzed. To the surprise of the entire scientific community, Miller was able to produce abundant molecules typical of modern cellular organisms, such as the amino acids alanine and aspartic acid, and other organic molecules such as urea and succinic acid.

*S. L. Miller, Science 117 (1953):528.

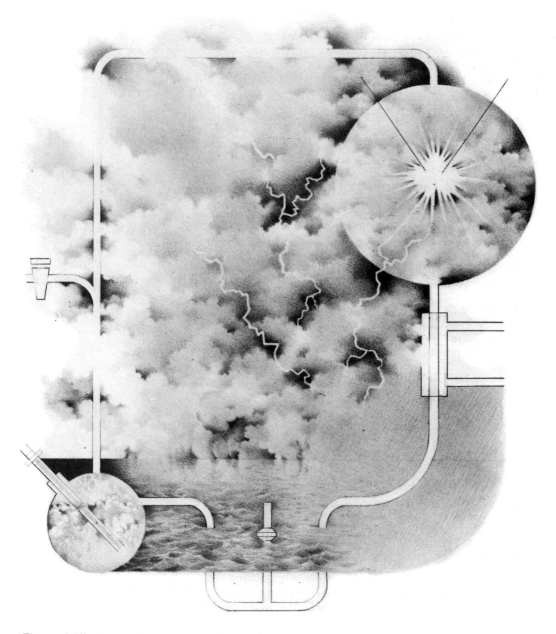

Fig. 11. Miller's experiment as
a metaphor of what occurred
in the primitive atmosphere.

fabric-making machine. The reason is that this
membrane not only limits the extension of the
transformation network that produced its own
components but it participates in this network. If
it did not have this spatial arrangement, cell metabolism would disintegrate in a molecular mess
that would spread out all over and would not constitute a discrete unity such as a cell.

What we have, then, is a unique situation as regards relations of chemical transformations: on
the one hand, we see a network of dynamic transformations that produces its own components
and that is essential for a boundary; on the other
hand, we see a boundary that is essential for the
operation of the network of transformations which
produced it as a unity:

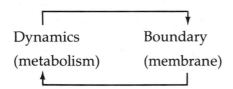

Dynamics   Boundary

(metabolism)   (membrane)

Note that these are not sequential processes,
but two different aspects of a unitary phenomenon. It is not that first there is a boundary, then a
dynamics, then a boundary, and so forth. We are
describing a type of phenomenon in which the
possibility of distinguishing one thing from a
whole (something you can see under the microscope, for instance) depends on the integrity of
the processes that make it possible. Interrupt (at
some point) the cellular metabolic network and
you will find that after a while you don't have any
more unity to talk about! The most striking feature of an autopoietic system is that it pulls itself
up by its own bootstraps and becomes distinct

Organization and Structure

Organization denotes those relations that must exist among the components of a system for it to be a member of a specific class. *Structure* denotes the components and relations that actually constitute a particular unity and make its organization real.

Thus, for instance, in a toilet the organization of the system of water-level regulation consists in the relations between an apparatus capable of detecting the water level and another apparatus capable of stopping the inflow of water. The toilet unit embodies a mixed system of plastic and metal comprising a float and a bypass valve. This specific structure, however, could be modified by replacing the plastic with wood, without changing the fact that there would still be a toilet organization.

from its environment through its own dynamics, in such a way that both things are inseparable.

Living beings are characterized by their autopoietic organization. They differ from each other in their structure, but they are alike in their organization.

Autonomy and Autopoiesis

By realizing what characterizes living beings in their autopoietic organization, we can unify a whole lot of empirical data about their biochemistry and cellular functioning. The concept of autopoiesis, therefore, does not contradict these data. Rather, it is supported by them; it explicitly proposes that such data be interpreted from a specific point of view which stresses that living beings are *autonomous* unities.

We use the word "autonomy" in its current

sense; that is, a system is autonomous if it can specify its own laws, what is proper to it. We are *not* proposing that living beings are the only autonomous entities. Certainly they are not. But one of the most evident features of a living being is its autonomy. We *are* proposing that the mechanism that makes living beings autonomous systems is autopoiesis. This characterizes them as autonomous systems.

The question about autonomy is as old as the question about the living. It is only contemporary biologists who feel uncomfortable over the question of how to understand the autonomy of the living. From our standpoint, however, this question is a guideline to understanding the autonomy of living beings: to understand them, we must understand the organization that defines them as unities. Being aware that living beings are autonomous unities helps to show how their autonomy—usually seen as mysterious and elusive—becomes explicit, for we realize that what defines them as unities is their autopoietic organization, and it is in this autopoietic organization that they become real and specify themselves at the same time.

Our intention, therefore, is to proceed scientifically: if we cannot provide a list that characterizes a living being, why not propose a system that generates all the phenomena proper to a living being? The evidence that an autopoietic unity has exactly all these features becomes evident in the light of what we know about the interdependence between metabolism and cellular structure.

That living beings have an organization, of course, is proper not only to them but also to everything we can analyze as a system. What is distinctive about them, however, is that their organization is such that their only product is themselves, with no separation between producer and product. The being and doing of an autopoieic unity are inseparable, and this is their specific mode of organization.

Like any organization, autopoietic organization can be attained by many different types of components. We have to realize, however, that as regards the molecular origin of terrestrial living beings, only certain molecular species probably possessed the characteristics required for autopoietic unities, thus initiating the structural history to which we ourselves belong. For instance, it was necessary to have molecules capable of forming membranes sufficiently stable and plastic to be, in turn, effective barriers, and to have changing properties for the diffusion of molecules and ions over long periods of time with respect to molecular speeds. Molecules from silicon layers, for instance, are too rigid for them to participate in dynamic unities (cells) in an ongoing and fast molecular interchange with the medium.

It was only at that point in the Earth's history when conditions were right for the forming of organic molecules such as proteins, which have enormous complexity and pliancy, that conditions were right also for the forming of autopoietic unities. In fact, we can assume that when all these sufficient conditions were present in the Earth's history, autopoietic systems formed inevitably.

That moment is the point we can refer to as the moment when life began. This does not mean that it happened in one instance and in one place only; nor can we specify a date for it. All the available evidence leads us to believe that once conditions were ripe for the origin of living systems, they

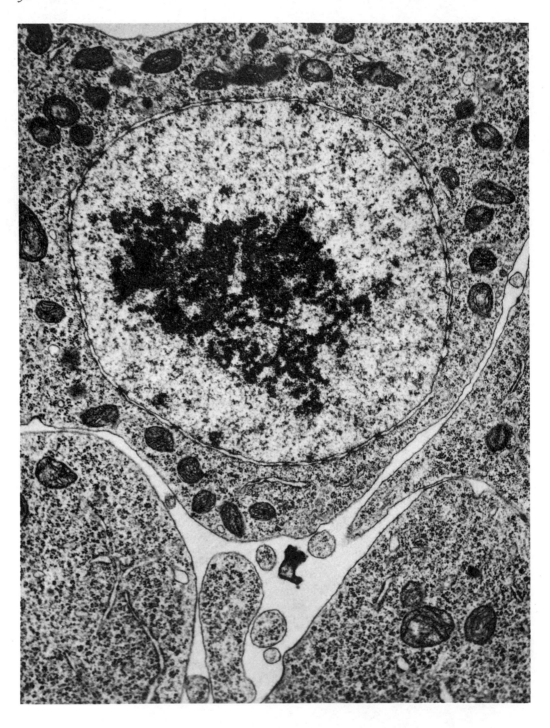

Cells and Their Membranes

The cell membrane plays a more sizable and varied role than that of a simple line of spatial demarcation for a number of chemical transformations, because it participates therein like other cellular components. This takes place under circumstances in which the cell interior has a rich architecture of large molecular blocks, through which pass many organic species in continuous exchange, and the membrane is operationally part of that interior. This is true both for the membranes which limit the cellular spaces that adjoin the exterior medium and for those membranes which limit each one of the different internal spaces of the cell (see accompanying figures).

This interior architecture and cell dynamics are complementary features of cellular autopoiesis.

Fig. 12. An electron micrograph of a cell specimen from a leech, showing membranes and intracellular components (magnified approximately 20,000 times).

originated many times; that is, many autopoietic unities with many structural variants emerged in many places on the Earth over a period of perhaps many millions of years.

The emergence of autopoietic unities on the face of the Earth is a landmark in the history of our solar system. We have to understand this well. The formation of a unity always determines a number of phenomena associated with the features that define it; we may thus say that each class of unities specifies a particular phenomenology. Thus, autopoietic unities specify biological phenomenology as the phenomenology proper of those unities with features distinct from physical phenomenology. This is so, not because autopoietic unities go against any aspect of physical phenomenology—since their molecular components must fulfill all physical laws—but because the phenomena they generate in functioning as autopoietic unities depend on their organization and the way this organization comes about, and not on the physical nature of their components (which only determine their space of existence).

Thus, if a cell interacts with molecule X and incorporates it in its processes, what takes place as a

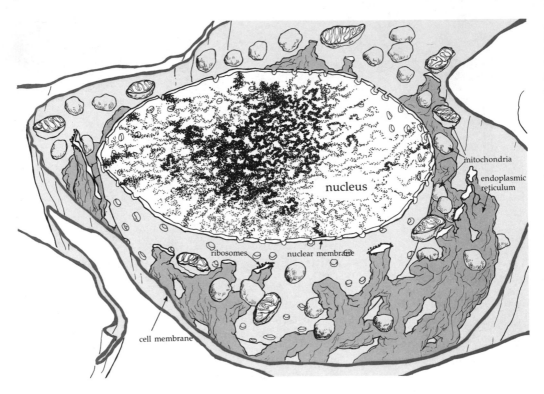

result of this interaction is determined not by the properties of molecule X but by the way in which that molecule is "seen" or taken by the cell as it incorporates the molecule in its autopoietic dynamics. The changes that occur therein as a result of this interaction will be those changes caused by the cell's own structure as a unity. Therefore, inasmuch as the autopoietic organization causes biologic phenomenology by bringing about living beings as autonomous unities, a biologic phenomenon will be any phenomenon that involves the autopoiesis of at least one living being.

Fig. 13. Diagram of the main profiles of the leech cell shown in Fig. 12, such as the nuclear membrane, mitochondria, endoplasmic reticulum, ribosomes, and cell membrane. Note sketch of hypothetical three-dimensional projection of what would be under the surface of the specimen.

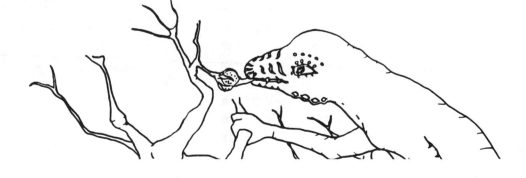

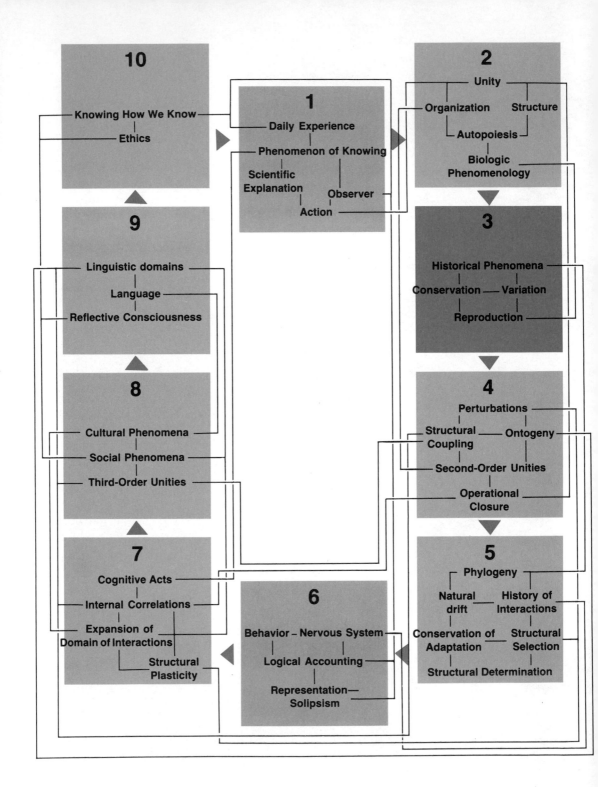

10

Knowing How We Know
Ethics

1

Daily Experience
Phenomenon of Knowing
Scientific
Explanation   Observer
Action

2

Unity
Organization   Structure
Autopoiesis

Biologic
Phenomenology

9

Linguistic domains
Language
Reflective Consciousness

3

Historical Phenomena
Conservation — Variation
Reproduction

8

Cultural Phenomena
Social Phenomena
Third-Order Unities

4

Perturbations
Structural   Ontogeny
Coupling
Second-Order Unities
Operational
Closure

7

Cognitive Acts
Internal Correlations
Expansion of
Domain of Interactions
Structural
Plasticity

6

Behavior – Nervous System
Logical Accounting
Representation—
Solipsism

5

Phylogeny
Natural   History of
drift   Interactions
Conservation of   Structural
Adaptation   Selection
Structural Determination

3   History: Reproduction and Heredity

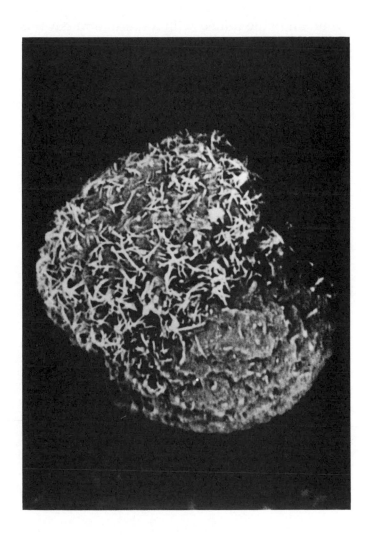

Fig. 14. One of the first divisions of a mouse embryo.

This chapter deals with reproduction and heredity. There are two compelling reasons for this. One of them is that as living beings (and, as we shall see, as social beings), we have a history: we are descendants by reproduction, not only of our human forebears but also of very different forebears who go back in the past more than 3 billion years. The other reason is that as organisms, we are multicellular beings and all our cells descend by reproduction from the particular cell formed when an ovule united with a sperm and gave us our origin. Reproduction is therefore inserted in our history in relation to ourselves as human beings and to our individual cell components. Oddly enough, this makes us and our cells beings of the same ancestral age. Moreover, from a historical standpoint, this is valid for all living beings and all contemporary cells: we share the same ancestral age. Hence, to understand living beings in all their dimensions, and thereby understand ourselves, we have to understand the mechanisms that make living beings historical beings. To this end, we shall examine first the phenomenon of reproduction.

Reproduction: What's It All About?

Biology has studied the process of reproduction from many points of view, particularly regarding cells. It has long since demonstrated that a cell can originate another cell through division. We speak of cell division (or mitosis) as a complex process of rearranging cellular elements that brings about a plane of division. What happens during this process? Reproduction generally consists in one unity, by some specific process, giving origin to

Historical Phenomena

Each time in a system that a state arises as a modification of a previous state, we have a *historical phenomenon*.

another unity of the same class; that is, it gives origin to another unity that an observer can recognize as possessing the same organization as the original one.

It is evident, therefore, that reproduction presupposes two basic conditions: an original unity and the process that reproduces it.

In the case of living beings, the original unity is a living being, an autopoietic unity; and the process—we shall say later exactly what it is—must end with the formation of at least one other autopoietic unity distinct from what is considered to be the first.

The careful reader must have realized by now that by looking at reproduction in this way, we are implying that it is *not* constitutive of living things and therefore (as should now be evident) does not play a part in their organization. We are so used to regarding living beings as a list of properties (and reproduction as one of them) that this may appear shocking on reflection. Nevertheless, what we are saying is simple: reproduction cannot be a part of the organization of living beings because to reproduce something, that something must *first* constitute a unity and have an organization that defines it. This is simple logic and we use it every

Organization and History

The dynamics of any system can be explained by showing the relations between its parts and the regularities of their interactions so as to reveal its organization. For us to fully understand it, however, we need not only to see it as a unity operating in its internal dynamics, but also to see it in its circumstances, i.e., in the context to which its operation connects it. This understanding requires that we adopt a certain distance for observation, a perspective that in the case of historical systems implies a reference to their origin. This can be easy, for instance, in the case of man-made machines, for we have access to every detail of their manufacture. The situation is not that easy, however, as regards living beings: their genesis and their history are never directly visible and can be reconstructed only by fragments.

day. Therefore, if we carry this ordinary logic to its consequences, we will be forced to conclude that in speaking of the reproduction of a living being, we are implying that it must be capable of existing without reproducing itself. It is enough to think of a mule to realize that this must be so. Now, what we are discussing in this chapter is how the structural dynamics of an autopoietic unity becomes complicated in the process of reproduction, and the consequences of this in the history of living beings. To *add* anything to a structural dynamics, however, is quite different from changing the essential characteristics of a unity; the latter implies changing its organization.

To understand what happens in cell reproduction, let us look at varied situations that give rise to unities of the same class.

Modes of Generating Unities

Replication We refer to replication (or, at times, production) whenever we have an operating mechanism that can repeatedly generate unities of the same class. For instance, a factory is a large productive mechanism which, by repeated application of one same process, turns out series of replicas of unities of the same class: fabrics, cars, tires (Fig. 15).

The same happens with cell components. We see this very clearly in protein production, where ribosomes, messenger and transfer nucleic acids, and other molecules constitute together the productive machinery and the proteins constitute the product.

Basic to the phenomenon of replication is the fact that the productive mechanism and the product are operationally different systems, and the productive mechanism generates elements independent of it. Note that as a consequence of how replication takes place, the unities produced are historically *independent* of each other. What happens to any one of them in its individual history does not affect what happens to those that follow in the series of production. What happens to my Toyota after I buy it in no way affects the Toyota factory, which will imperturbably continue producing its automobiles. In short, unities produced by replication do not constitute among themselves a historical system.

Copy We speak of a copy whenever we have a model unity and a projective procedure for generating an identical unity. For instance, this page put through a Xerox machine yields what we call a copy. Hence, the model unity is this page, and the process is the method of operating with an optically projective mechanism (the Xerox machine).

Fig. 15. A case of replication.

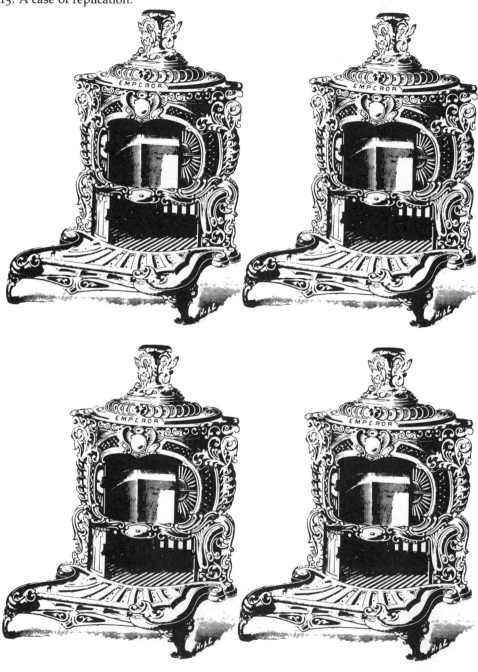

Now, we can distinguish in this situation two basically different cases. If the *same* model is used to make many successive copies, we have a number of copies historically independent of each other. But if the result of one copy is used as a model to make the following copy, a number of historically connected unities are generated, for what happens to each of them during the time they become individual, before being used as a model, determines the characteristics of the following copy. Thus, if a Xerox copy of this page is copied in turn by the same machine, it is clear that the original and the two copies differ slightly from each other. If we repeat this same process, at the end of many copies, as is obvious, we can note the progressive transformation of those copies into a lineage or historical succession of copied unities. A creative use of this historical phenomenon is what is known in art as anamorphosis (Fig. 16). This is an excellent example of historical drift.

Reproduction We speak of reproduction when a unity undergoes a *fracture* that results in two unities of the same class. This happens, for instance, when a piece of chalk is broken in two or when a bunch of grapes is broken into two bunches of grapes. The resulting unities are not identical with the original one nor are they identical with each other; however, they belong to the same class as the original; that is, they have the same organization. Such is not the case when a radio or a check is fractured. In these cases, fracture of the original unity destroys it and leaves two fragments, not two unities of the same class as the original one.

In order for a fracture to result in reproduction, the structure of the unity must be organized in a *distributed* and noncompartmentalized way. Thus, the plane of fracture separates fragments with structures capable of embodying independently the same original organization. The chalk and the bunch of grapes have this type of structure and admit many planes of fracture, because their organization includes all their components repeating themselves in a distributed and noncompartmentalized way throughout their extension (calcium crystals in chalk and grapes in a bunch).

Many systems in nature satisfy these requisites; hence, reproduction is a frequent phenomenon. Examples are mirrors, sticks, communities, and roads (Fig. 17). On the other hand, a radio and a coin do not reproduce, because their defining relations are not repeated in their respective extensions. There are many systems in this class, such as cups, persons, fountain pens, and a declaration of human rights. This incapacity to reproduce is a frequent pattern in the universe. Interestingly, reproduction as a phenomenon is not confined to a

particular space or to a particular group of systems. The core of the reproductive process (unlike replication or copy) is that everything happens in the unity as *part* of the unity, and there is no separation between the reproducing system and the reproduced system. Nor can it be said that the unities resulting from reproduction preexist or are being formed before the reproductive fracture occurs. They simply do not exist. Further, although the unities resulting from the reproductive fracture have the same organization as the original unity and therefore have structural aspects similar to it, they have structural aspects also different from it and from one another. This is so not only because they are smaller but also because their structures derive directly from the structure of the original unity at the time of reproduction; and when forming, they receive different components of the original unity which are not uniformly distributed and which are a function of its individual history of structural change.

Fig. 16. A case of copy with replacement of model.

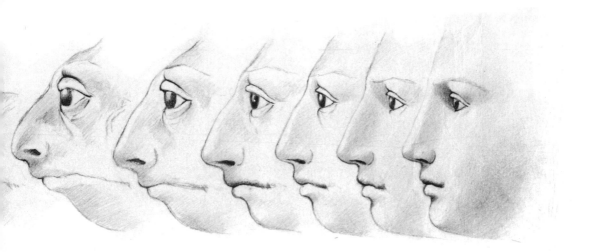

Fig. 17. A case of reproduction by fracture.

Because of these characteristics, reproduction *necessarily* gives origin to historically connected unities. If these unities suffer reproductive fractures, they form together a historical system.

Cell Reproduction

What's all this about cells? If we take any cell in its interphase stage—that is, not during its reproductive process—and we fracture it, we do not get two cells. During interphase, a cell is a compartmentalized system; that is, there are components that are segregated from the rest or are present in a single quantity (which rules out any plane of reproductive fracture). This is the case particularly with deoxyribonucleic acids (DNA), which are part of chromosomes and, during interphase, are separated from the cytoplasm in the nucleus by the nuclear membrane (Fig. 18a).

During mitosis or cell division, all the occurring processes (b–j) consist of cell decompartmentalization. This is readily seen in Figure 18, which shows the dissolution of nuclear membrane (with replication of the large double helixes of DNA) and the displacement of chromosomes and other components. This makes possible a plane of fracture. Now, all this occurs as a result of cellular autopoiesis, and without interrupting it. Thus, part of the very dynamics of the cell leads to structural changes such as the forming of a mitotic spindle (d–h). These changes bring about a cleavage or fracture of the cell thus formed.

Viewed in this way, the process of cell reproduction is simple: a fracture in a plane that generates two unities of the same class. In modern eukaryotic cells (with nucleus) this plane and the mechanics of the fracture are established by an intricate and exquisite mechanism of molecular choreography. In ancient (or prokaryotic) cells that do not show compartmentalization as in Figure 18, the process is actually simpler. In any case, cell reproduction is clearly reproduction in the sense discussed before, not replication or a copy of unities.

Unlike the examples of reproduction given before, however, cell reproduction presents a special phenomenon: autopoietic dynamics is what makes cellular fracture take place in the reproductive plane. No external agent or force is needed. We can presume that such was not the case with the first autopoietic unities and that, in fact, reproduction was first a fragmentation that resulted from the bumping of these unities with other external entities. In the historical network thus produced, some odd cells underwent reproductive fracture as a result of their internal dynamics. These variants possessed a dividing mechanism from which derived a lineage or stable historical succession. It is not clear how this occurred. These origins are probably forever lost to us. But this does not invalidate the fact that cell division is a special case of reproduction that we can legitimately call self-reproduction.

Fig. 18. Mitosis or reproduction by fracture in an animal cell. The diagram shows the different stages of decompartmentalization, which makes the reproductive fracture possible.

f

e

d

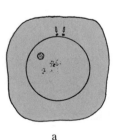

a

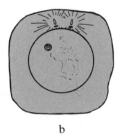

b

c

Reproductive Heredity

Independently of how it begins, each time there is a historical series, we have the phenomenon of heredity; that is, we find structural configurations proper to a member of one series that reappear in the following member. This is evident both in the embodiment of the organization proper to the class and in other individual characteristics. If we reflect on the case of the historical series of successive Xerox copies, we find that however different the first copies are from the last ones, certain black-and-white relations in the letters will not change; this makes it possible for us to read them and to say that one is a copy of the other. Precisely at the time when the copy becomes so hazy that we cannot read it, the historical lineage will be ended.

Likewise, in those systems that reproduce, heredity is present in each reproductive instance, as a constitutive phenomenon of reproduction, by the mere fact that two unities of the same class are generated. In other words, precisely because reproduction occurs when there is a plane of fracture in a unity of distributed structure, there will necessarily be a certain permanence of structural configurations from one generation to the next.

And in the same way, since reproductive frac-

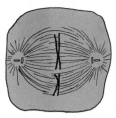

g

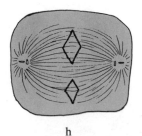

h

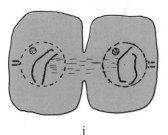

i

j

k

Heredity

Heredity means the transgenerational conservation of any structural aspect in a lineage of historically connected unities.

ture results in the separation of two unities with the same organization but with different structures of the original unity, it conserves organization and gives rise to structural variation. The phenomenon of reproduction necessarily implies the generation both of similarities and of structural differences between "parents," "children," and "siblings." Those aspects of the initial structure of the new unity which we evaluate as identical to the original unity are called *heredity;* those aspects of the initial structure of the new unity which we evaluate as different from the original unity are called reproductive *variation.* For this reason, each new unity invariably begins its individual history with structural similarities and differences in respect to its forebears. These similarities and differences, as we shall see, will be conserved or lost depending on the circumstances of the respective ontogenies. Right now, we wish to stress only that the phenomenon of heredity and the production of structural changes in descendants is proper of reproduction; it is not less valid in the reproduction of living beings.

In cell reproduction there are many instances where it is possible to detect with precision the structural circumstances that bring about both variation and conservation of similarities. Thus, some components admit few variations in their way of participating in autopoiesis, but they admit many ways of participating in the cellular dynamics. Such components participate in basic structural configurations that are conserved from generation to generation (otherwise there is no reproduction) with only slight changes.

The best known of these components are the DNA (nucleic acids) or genes, whose basic structure is replicated in reproduction with little change. This results in large-scale conservation among individuals of one lineage; at the same time, there is continual variation of structural aspects that do not remain constant for more than one or two generations. Thus, for example, the mode of synthesis of proteins with the participa-

The Notion of Genetic Information

We have often heard it said that genes contain the "information" that specifies a living being. This is wrong for two basic reasons. First, because it confuses the phenomenon of heredity with the mechanism of replication of certain cell components (DNA), whose structure has great transgenerational stability. And second, because when we say that DNA contains what is necessary to specify a living being, we divest these components (part of the autopoietic network) of their interrelation with the rest of the network. It is the network of interactions in its entirety that constitutes and specifies the characteristics of a particular cell, and not one of its components. That modifications in those components called genes dramatically affect the structure is very certain. The error lies in confusing essential participation with unique responsibility. By the same token one could say that the political constitution of a country determines its history. This is obviously absurd. The political constitution is an essential component in any history but it does not contain the "information" that specifies that history.

tion of DNA has remained unchanged through many lineages, but the type of proteins synthesized has changed very much in the history of those lineages.

The pattern of distribution of structural variance or invariance along a system of lineages determines the different ways in which heredity appears to be distributed from generation to generation and which we see as different genetic (hereditary) systems. Modern studies in genetics have centered mainly on the genetics of nuclear acids. There are other genetic (hereditary) systems, however, that we are just beginning to understand. They have been obscured by the genetics of nucleic acids, like those associated with other cellular compartments such as mitochondria and membranes.

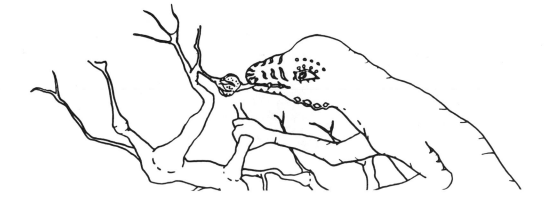

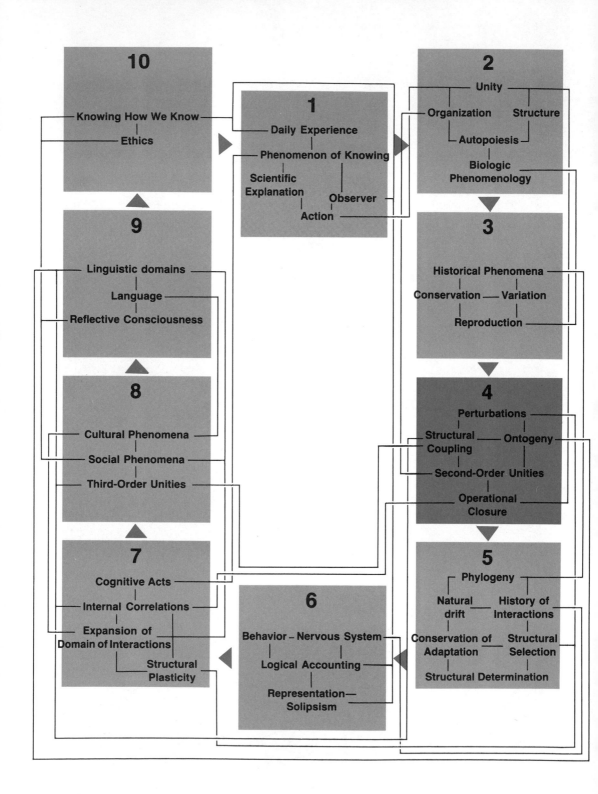

4　The Life of Metacellulars

Fig. 19. *Water* by
G. Arcimboldo.

Ontogeny is the history of structural change in a
unity without loss of organization in that unity.
This ongoing structural change occurs in the unity
from moment to moment, either as a change triggered by interactions coming from the environment in which it exists or as a result of its internal
dynamics. As regards its continuous interactions
with the environment, the cell unity classifies
them and sees them in accordance with its structure at every instant. That structure, in turn,
continuously changes because of its internal dynamics. The overall result is that the ontogenic
transformation of a unity ceases only with its disintegration. To abbreviate this situation, when we
refer to autopoietic unities, we shall use the following diagram:

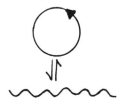

Now, what happens when we consider the ontogeny of, not one, but two (or more) neighboring
unities in their medium of interaction? We can abbreviate this situation as follows:

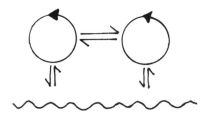

Structural Coupling

We can look at this situation, of course, from the perspective of either one of the unities, and it will be symmetrical. This means that, for the cell on the left, the one on the right is only one more source of interactions, indistinguishable from those which we, as observers, classify as coming from the "inert" environment. Conversely, for the cell on the right, the other is one more source of interactions encountered according to its own structure.

This means that two (or more) autopoietic unities can undergo coupled ontogenies when their interactions take on a *recurrent* or more stable nature. We have to keep this clearly in mind. Every ontogeny occurs within an environment; we, as observers, can describe both as having a particular structure such as diffusion, secretion, temperature. In describing autopoietic unity as having a particular structure, it will become clear to us that the interactions (as long as they are recurrent) between unity and environment will consist of reciprocal perturbations. In these interactions, the structure of the environment only *triggers* structural changes in the autopoietic unities (it does not specify or direct them), and vice versa for the environment. The result will be a history of mutual congruent structural changes as long as the autopoietic unity and its containing environment do not disintegrate: there will be a *structural coupling*.

Structural Coupling

We speak of structural coupling whenever there is a history of recurrent interactions leading to the structural congruence between two (or more) systems.

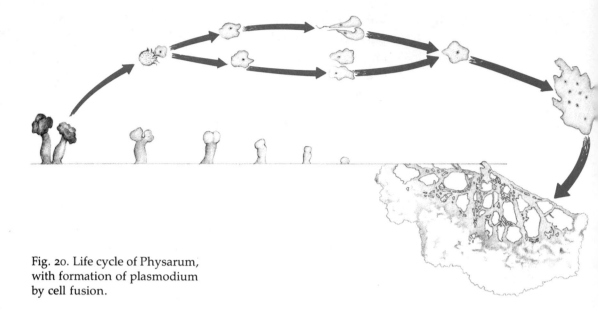

Fig. 20. Life cycle of Physarum,
with formation of plasmodium
by cell fusion.

Among all possible interactions between systems, there are some that are particularly recurrent or repetitive. For instance, if we look at the
membrane of a cell, we note that there is a constant active transport of certain ions (such as sodium or calcium) through that cell, in such a way
that in the presence of those ions the cell reacts by
embodying them in its metabolic network. This
active ionic transport occurs regularly; and we, as
observers, can say that the structural coupling
of the cells with their medium or environment
enables these cells to interact recurrently with
the ions that they contain. The cellular structural
coupling enables these interactions to take place
only in certain ions, for if other ions (cesium or
lithium, for instance) are introduced into the medium, the structural changes that these ions would
unleash in the cell will interrupt its autopoiesis.

Now, why is it that autopoiesis occurs in each cellular type with the participation of only a certain kind of regular and recurrent interaction and not of others? This question can be answered only by referring to the phylogeny or history of the corresponding cellular strain; that is, the type of current structural coupling of each cell is the present state of the history of structural transformations of the phylogeny to which it belongs. In other words, it is a moment in the natural drift of that lineage which results from the conservation of the structural coupling of the previous cells in the lineage. Thus, for the example given before, in the present state of that cellular natural drift the membranes operate by transporting sodium and calcium ions, and not others.

The structural coupling with the medium as a condition of existence covers all possible cellular interactions. Therefore, it includes interactions with other cells as well. The cells of multicellular systems normally exist only by taking other cells in close cellular proximity as a medium for realizing their autopoiesis. Those systems are the result of the natural drift of lineages in which this close proximity has been conserved.

A group of single-cell organisms called myxomycetes are an excellent source of examples that reveal this clearly. Thus, when a spore of *Physarum* germinates, it gives origin to a cell (Fig. 20, top). If the environment is humid, the cell grows a flagellum and becomes motile. If the environment is dry, the cell develops pseudopods and becomes an amoeba. These two kinds of cells eventually divide and give rise to many other cells; in the closeness of their structural coupling, these cells fuse together and form a plasmodium, which in turn forms a macroscopic fructiferous body that produces spores. (Note the drawing in Fig. 21, where the upper part has a greater enlargement than the lower part.)

In these phylogenetically old eukaryotes, the close cellular aggregation culminates in a new unity when the fructiferous body forms as a result of cellular fusion. This fructiferous body actually constitutes a metacellular unit, whose existence is historically complemented by the cells that give origin to it in the completion of the *life cycle* of the organic unity to which it belongs (and which is defined by that life cycle). And here is what we must carefully bear in mind: the formation of metacellular units capable of giving origin to lineages by reproducing through single cells originates a phenomenology different from the phenomenology of the cells that make them up. This metacellular or *second-order unity* will have a structural coupling and ontogeny adequate to its structure as a composite unity. In particular, metacellular systems such as the one described

Fig. 21. Life cycle of *Dycostelium* (lime fungus), with fructiferous body formed by the grouping of cells that result from the reproduction of a founding spore cell.

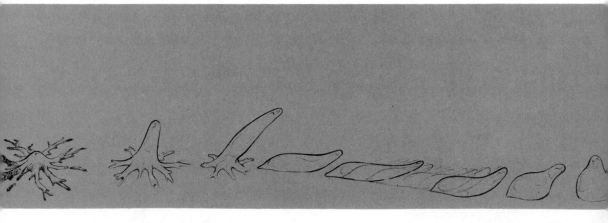

before will have a macroscopic ontogeny, and not a microscopic one like that of its cells.

A more intricate example is that of another myxomycete: *Dycostelium* (Fig. 21).[1] In this group, when the environment has certain special features, amoeboid individuals are capable of aggregating to form a fructiferous body as in the foregoing example, but without cellular fusion. Also in this group, however, we find that second-order unities show a clear diversity of cellular types. Thus, the cells at the upper end of the fructiferous body generate spores, whereas the cells at the base do not. These become full of vacuoles and walls, which gives a mechanical support to the entire metacellular system. Here we see that in the dynamism of this close cellular aggregation in a life cycle, the structural changes that each cell undergoes in its history of interactions with other cells are complementary to each other, within the constraints of their participation in the metacellular unity they comprise. This is why the ontogenic structural changes of each cell necessarily differ,

1. J. T. Bonner, *Proceedings of the National Academy of Science USA* 45(1959):379.

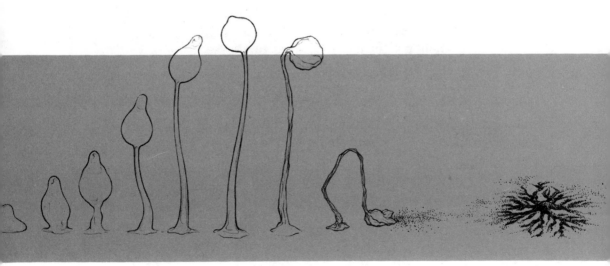

depending on how they participate in the constitution of that unity through their interactions and
neighboring relations.

Life Cycles

We stress that the close aggregation of cells descending from a single cell that results in a metacellular unity is a condition wholly consistent with
the continuous autopoiesis of those cells. Such cellular aggregation, however, is not biologically
necessary inasmuch as many living beings have remained unicellular organisms in the long history of
their existence. In those lineages where cellular aggregation *has* occurred, the consequences for the
respective histories of structural transformations
are profound. Let us take a closer look at this
situation.

The ontogeny of a metacellular system is evidently going to be determined by the domain of
interactions that it specifies as a total unity, and
not by the individual interactions of the component cells. In other words, the life of a multicellular individual as a unity goes on through
the operation of its components, but it is not determined by their properties. Each one of these
pluricellular individuals, however, results from
the division and segregation of a lineage of cells
that originate at the moment of fertilization of a
single cell or zygote produced by some of the
organs or parts of a multicellular organism. If
there is no generation of new individuals, no continuity of lineage is possible. And for there to be
new individuals, their beginnings must trace back
to one cell. It is as simple as this: the logic of the
constitution of each metacellular organism de-

mands that it be part of a cycle in which there is a necessary unicellular stage.

It is during the unicellular reproductive phase of a multicellular organism when generational changes occur. Therefore, there is no difference in the way lineages are established in multicellular and unicellular organisms. In other words, the life cycle of a metacellular organism constitutes a unity in which the ontogeny of the organism occurs in its transformation from unicellular to multicellular, but in which reproduction and reproductive changes occur during the unicellular phase.

All known multicellular living beings are elaborate variations of the same theme: cellular organization and the constitution of a phylogeny. Each multicellular individual represents an elaborate moment in the ontogeny of a lineage whose changes continue to be cellular. In this regard, multicellularity does not introduce anything fundamentally new. The novelty about it consists in that it makes possible many different classes of individuals, for it makes possible many different lineages as distinct ways of conserving ontogenic structural coupling in the environment. The rich diversity of living beings on earth, including us, is due to the appearance of this multicellular variant within cellular lineages.

Note, however, that sexual reproduction of multicellular organisms does not alter the basic characterization of reproduction that we saw in the last chapter. In effect, sexual reproduction requires that one of the cells of the multicellular organism take on an independent operational dynamics (like the sperm) and fuse with another cell of another organism of the same class, to form the zygote that is the unicellular phase of that living being. There are some multicellular organisms that can also or exclusively reproduce by simple fracture. When this occurs, the unity of variation in the lineage is not a cell but an organism.

The consequences of sexual reproduction are seen in the rich structural recombination that results from it. This makes possible, on the one hand, the intercrossing of reproductive lineages and, on the other hand, a very great increase in the structural changes possible in each reproductive instance. In this way, genetics and heredity are enriched by effects that combine the structural alternatives of a group of living beings. This effect of increasing variability, which in turn makes phylogenetic drift possible (as we shall see in the next chapter), explains why sexuality is practically universal among living beings while it facilitates the branching of lineages.

Tempo of Transformations

A splendid way to look at metacellular systems and their life cycles is to compare the time it takes them to cover a complete life cycle, depending on their size.[2] Thus, for instance, Figure 22a depicts the cycle of a myxomycete (which we discussed before), showing at one axis the time that each stage takes to reach completion and, at the other axis, the size attained. Thus, it takes more or less one day for a 1-centimeter-long fructiferous body to form. The spore, measuring some 10 millionths of a meter, forms in about one minute. Figure 22b depicts the same history, this time of a frog. The zygote, which gives origin to an adult, forms in more or less one minute, whereas the adult takes

2. J. T. Bonner, *Size and Cycle* (Princeton, N.J.: Princeton University Press, 1965).

nearly a year to grow several centimeters. The same applies to the biggest tree in the world, the sequoia; it grows to a height of over 300 feet during a formation time of one thousand years (Fig. 22c). It applies also to the largest animal in the world, the blue whale, which grows to a length of nearly 45 yards in ten years (Fig. 22d).

Independently of size and outward appearance, in all these cases the stages are always the same: from an initial cell, the process of cellular division and differentiation generates a second-order individual through coupling between the cells resulting from those cellular divisions. The individual thus formed has an ontogeny, varying in extension, which reaches the next reproductive stage with the formation of a new zygote. In this way the generational cycle is a basic unit that is both conserved and transformed in time. One way of making this clear is to note on a graph the reproduction time in relation to the size (Fig. 23). A bacterium that is unicellular has a very rapid reproduction. Hence, its rhythm of transformation is rapid. One necessary effect of the formation of second-order individuals by cellular aggregation is that time is needed for cellular growth and differentiation; therefore, frequency of generations will be much less.

This graph makes it clear that there is a very great similarity among multicellulars, as there is among cells. In spite of their amazing and apparent diversity, they all conserve reproduction through a unicellular stage as a central feature of their identity as biologic systems. This common element in their organization does not interfere with their great diversity, because this takes place in structural variation. The situation does permit

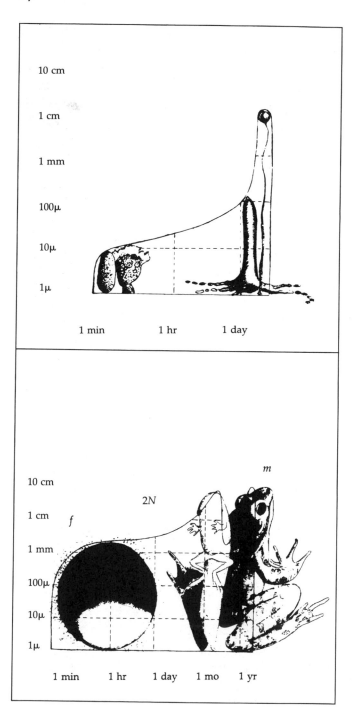

Fig. 22. Examples of the relation between the size reached and time needed to reach it in the different stages of the life cycles of four organisms.

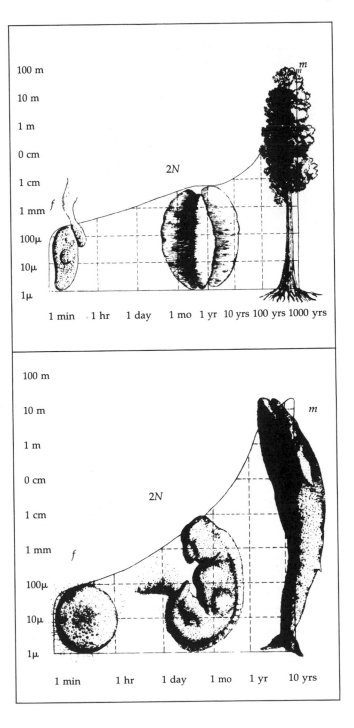

us, however, to see that all this variation is a variation around a fundamental type, which results in
different ways of bringing forth the world by different units that have the same organization. That
is to say, every ontogenic variation results in different ways of being in the world, because it is the
structure of the unity that determines its interaction in the environment and the world it lives in.

Fig. 23. Time of transformation into unicellular and
metacellular organisms.

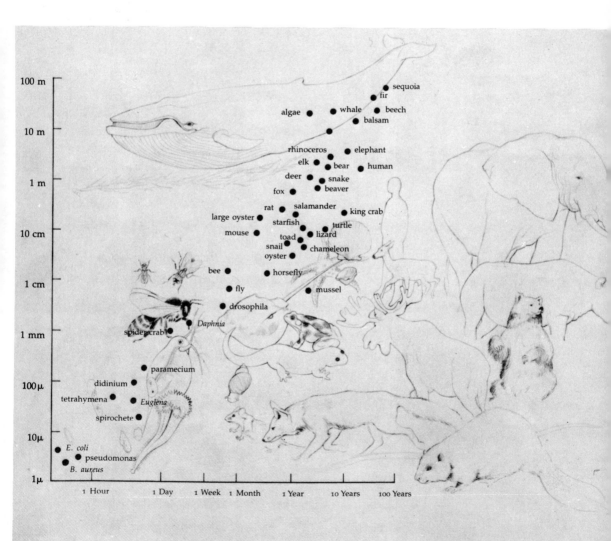

Metacellularity and the Nervous System

We have maintained in this book that it is not possible to understand how the nervous system works and therefore to understand the biology of cognition without understanding *where* the nervous system works. The cellular differentiation proper to metacellular organisms, with and without a nervous system, has a common logic present also in the makeup of the nervous system. A blue whale has billions of cells, but they are all reciprocally coupled, which makes possible this second-order unity, namely, the blue whale. Similarly, the nervous system contains millions of cells, but all are integrated as components of the organism. Losing sight of the organic roots of the nervous system is one of the major sources of confusion when we try to understand its effective operation. This will be the topic of a later chapter.

The Organization of Metacellulars

We speak of metacellulars when we refer to any unity in whose structure we can distinguish cell aggregates in close coupling. Metacellularity is present in all the major kingdoms of living beings: monera, protoctists, animals, plants, and fungi. Metacellularity has been a structural possibility from the earliest history of living beings.[3]

Now, what is common to all metacellulars in the five kingdoms is that they include cells as components of their structure. That is why we say that metacellulars are *second-order autopoietic systems*. But then we ask: what is the organization of metacellulars? Since component cells can be related in many different ways, it is evident that metacellulars admit different types of organization, for example, organisms, colonies, and societies. But are some metacellulars autopoietic unities? That is, are second-order autopoietic systems *also* first-order autopoietic systems? Is the fructiferous body of a myxomycete an autopoietic unity? How about the whale?

3. L. Margulis and K. Schwartz, *Five Kingdoms* (San Francisco: Freeman, 1982).

Symbiosis and Metacellularity

What we said in this chapter can be summed up by pointing out that if two autopoietic unities operate in a domain of structural coupling through recurrent interactions, diagrammatically as follows:

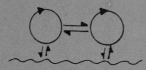

structural coupling through recurrent interactions may drift in two directions:

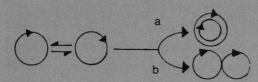

One direction is (a) toward inclusion of the boundaries of both unities; this situation leads to what is currently known as symbiosis. Symbiosis seems to have been very significant in the transition from auto-

poietic systems without internal compartments, or prokaryotes, to cells with internal compartments, or eukaryotes (see Fig. 14).* In effect, all cell organelles (e.g., mitochondria, chloroplasts, and even the nucleus) seem to have derived from ancestors that were once independent prokaryotes.

But it is the other alternative (b), diagrammed above, which is of particular interest to us in this chapter: the recurrent coupling in which the participating cells can preserve their individual limits, at the same time as they establish, by their coupling, a special new coherence which we distinguish as a metacellular unity and which we see as their form.

*L. Margulis, *Symbiosis in Cell Evolution* (San Francisco: Freeman, 1980).

These questions are sticklers. We know in great detail how a cell comes about as a molecular autopoietic unity, but how can we possibly describe in an organism the components and relations that make it a molecular autopoietic system? In the case of metacellulars, we are still ignorant of the molecular processes that would constitute those metacellulars as autopoietic unities comparable to cells.

For the purposes of this book, we shall leave open the question of whether or not metacellular systems are first-order autopoietic systems. What we can say is that they have *operational closure* in their organization: their identity is specified by a network of dynamic processes whose effects do not leave that network. But regarding the explicit form of that organization, we shall not speak further. This does not constitute a limitation, however, for our purposes here. As we already said, whatever the organization of metacellulars may be, they are made up of first-order autopoietic systems and form lineages by reproducing through cells. These two conditions are sufficient to assure us that whatever happens in them, as autonomous unities, happens with conservation of the autopoiesis of their component cells, as also with conservation of their own organization. Consequently, everything we are going to say will apply both to first- and second-order autopoietic systems; we shall make no distinction between them unless it is strictly necessary.

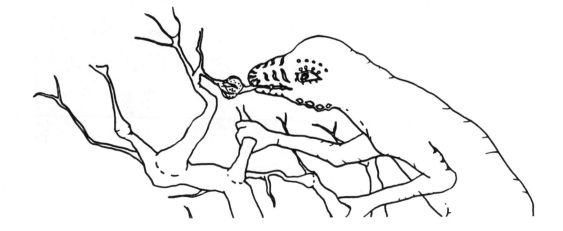

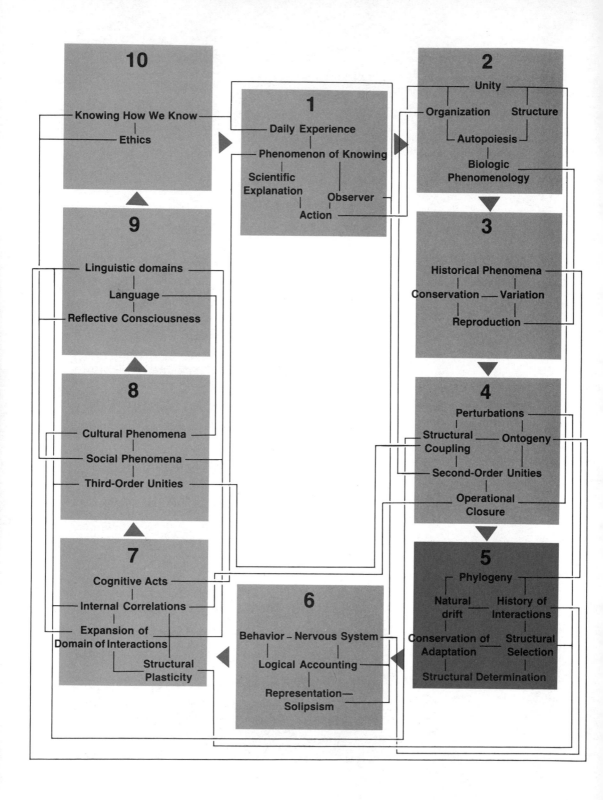

5   The Natural Drift of Living Beings

Fig. 24. Charles Darwin.

The preceding chapters have given us an idea of
three basic aspects of living beings. First, we have
seen how they are constituted as unities, how
their identity is defined by their autopoietic organization. Second, we have stated in what way
autopoietic systems can undergo sequential reproduction and thus generate a historical system
of lineages. Lastly, we have seen how multicellular organisms like ourselves are born from
the coupling of cells descending from a single cell
and how every metacellular organism, as one
element in generational cycles that always go
through a multicellular stage, is but a variation on
the same theme.

All this results in ontogenies of living beings
capable of reproduction and phylogenies of different reproductive lineages that intertwine in a
gigantic and diverse historical network. This is
clear in the organic surrounding world of plants,
animals, fungi, and bacteria, as also in the differences we observe between ourselves as human beings and other living beings. This great network
of historical transformations of living beings is
the warp and woof of their existence as historical
beings. In this chapter we shall go over some
topics that arise from the foregoing chapters, to
understand this *organic evolution* in a general and
global way, for without an adequate understanding of the historical mechanisms of structural
transformation there is no understanding of the
phenomenon of cognition. Actually, the key to
understanding the origin of evolution lies in something which we noted in the earlier chapters: the
inherent association between differences and
similarities in each reproductive stage, conservation of organizations, and structural change. Because there are similarities, there is the possibility

of a historical series or uninterrupted lineage. Because there are structural differences, there is the possibility of historical variations in the lineages. But, more precisely, how is it that certain lineages are produced or established and others are not? How is it that, when we look around, fish seem to us so naturally aquatic and horses so naturally adapted to the plains? To answer these questions, we must look more closely and explicitly at how interactions occur between living beings and their environment.

Structural Determination and Coupling

Ontogeny is the history of structural changes in a particular living being. In this history each living being begins with an initial structure. This structure conditions the course of its interactions and restricts the structural changes that the interactions may trigger in it. At the same time, it is born in a particular place, in a medium that constitutes the ambience in which it emerges and in which it interacts. This ambience appears to have a structural dynamics of its own, *operationally distinct* from the living being. This is a crucial point. As observers, we have distinguished the living system as a unity from its background and have characterized it as a definite organization. We have thus distinguished two structures that are going to be considered operationally independent of each other: living being and environment. Between them there is a necessary structural congruence (or the unity disappears). In the interactions between the living being and the environment within this structural congruence, the perturbations of the environment do not determine what happens to the living being; rather, it is the structure of the living being that determines what change occurs in it. This interaction is not instructive, for it does not determine what its effects are going to be. Therefore, we have used the expression "to trigger" an effect. In this way we refer to the fact that the changes that result from the interaction between the living being and its environment are brought about by the disturbing agent but *determined by the structure of the disturbed system.* The same holds true for the environment: the living being is a source of perturbations and not of instructions.

Now, at this point the reader may be thinking that all this sounds too complicated and that it is unique to living beings. To be exact, as in the case of reproduction, this is not a phenomenon unique to living beings. It takes place in all interactions. And if we do not see it in all its generality, it becomes a source of confusion. Hence, let us dwell a moment further on examining what happens each time we distinguish a unity and an environment in which it interacts.

The key to understanding all this is indeed simple: as scientists, we can deal only with unities that are *structurally determined.* That is, we can deal only with systems in which all their changes are determined by their structure, whatever it may be, and in which those structural changes are a result of their own dynamics or triggered by their interactions. In our daily lives, in fact, we behave as though all things we encounter are structurally determined unities. An automobile, a tape recorder, a sewing machine, and a computer are all systems we treat as though they were determined by their structure. Otherwise, how could we explain that when we find a breakdown we try to change the structure and not something else? If we step on the gas pedal of our car and the car doesn't move, it will never occur to us that there is something wrong with our pressing foot. We assume that the problem lies in the connection between the gas pedal and the injection system, that is, in the structure of the car. Thus, breakdowns in man-made machines reveal more about their effective operation than our descriptions of them when they operate normally. In the absence of failure, we sum up our description by saying that we "instruct" the computer to give us the balance of our bank account.

This everyday attitude (which becomes more systematic and explicit only in science, by rigorous application of the criterion of validation of scientific statements) is not only adequate for artificial systems but also for living beings and social systems. Otherwise we would never go to a doctor when we felt sick or replace a manager in a company when his performance does not meet expectations. We may choose not to explain many phenomena of our human experience; however, if we wish to explain them scientifically, we must treat the subject phenomena as being structurally determined.

All this becomes explicit when we distinguish four domains (classes) that the structure of a unity specifies:

a. *Domain of changes of state:* viz., all those structural changes that a unity can undergo without a change in its organization, i.e., with conservation of class identity

b. *Domain of destructive changes:* all those structural changes that a unity can undergo with loss of organization and therefore with loss of class identity

c. *Domain of perturbations:* all those interactions that trigger changes of state

d. *Domain of destructive interactions:* all those perturbations that result in a destructive change

Thus, we all reasonably suppose that lead bullets fired at someone at point-blank range trigger in the victim destructive changes specified by the

Fig. 25. The trumpet, like every unity, has its four domains: (a) of changes of state, (b) of destructive changes, (c) of perturbations, and (d) of destructive interactions.

structure of that person. As we well know, however, those same bullets are a mere perturbation for the structure of a vampire. He requires a wooden stake in his heart before he undergoes a destructive change. Moreover, it is obvious that a compact car crashing into a tree may undergo a destructive interaction, but this would be a mere perturbation for a tank (Fig. 25).

Note that in a dynamic system structurally determined, since the structure is in ongoing change, its structural domains will also change, although they will be specified at every moment by their present structure. This ongoing change in its structural domains is what is proper of the ontogeny of each dynamic unity, whether it is a cassette player or a leopard.

As long as a unity does not enter into a destructive interaction with its environment, we as observers will necessarily see between the structure of the environment and that of the unity a compatibility or congruence. As long as this compatibility exists, environment and unity act as mutual sources of perturbation, triggering changes of state. We have called this ongoing process "structural coupling." Thus, for example, in the history of structural coupling between the lineages of automobiles and cities there are dramatic changes on both sides, which have taken place in each one as an expression of its own structural dynamics under selective interactions with the other.

Ontogeny and Selection

Everything said before is valid for any system; therefore, it is valid also for living beings. Living beings are not unique in their determination nor in their structural coupling. What is proper to them, however, is that structural determination and coupling in them take place within the framework of ongoing conservation of the autopoiesis that defines them, whether of the first or second order, and that everything in them is subordinate to that conservation. Thus, even the autopoiesis of the cells that make up a metacellular system is subordinate to its autopoiesis as a second-order autopoietic system. Therefore, every structural change occurs in a living being necessarily limited by the conservation of its autopoiesis; and those interactions that trigger in it structural changes compatible with that conservation are perturbations, whereas those that do not are destructive interactions. Ongoing structural change of living beings with conservation of their autopoiesis is occurring at every moment, continuously, in many ways at the same time. It is the throbbing of all life.

Now, let us note something interesting: when we as observers speak of what happens to an organism in a specific interaction, we are in a peculiar situation. On the one hand, we have access to the structure of the environment and, on the other hand, to the structure of the organism; and we can consider the many ways in which both could have changed in their encounter, if the interactions had been different from those which actually occurred. We can thus imagine what the world would have been if Cleopatra had been ugly. Or, in a more serious vein, what that boy who begs alms from us would have been had he been properly fed as an infant. From this perspective, the structural changes that occur in a unity appear as "selected" by the environment through a continuous chain of interactions. Consequently,

Dangerous Curve: Natural Selection

The word "selection" is tricky in this context. We have to be careful not to slide unwittingly into a number of connotations that apply to other domains and not to the phenomenon at hand. In effect, we often think of the process of selection as the act of choosing voluntarily from among many alternatives. And it is tempting for us to believe that something similar occurs here, too: through its perturbations, the environment is supposedly "choosing" which of many possible changes are taking place.

This is completely the opposite of what actually occurs and contradictory to the fact that we are dealing with structurally determined systems. An interaction cannot specify a structural change, because that change is determined by the previous state of the subject unity and not by the structure of the disturbing agent, as we discussed in the previous section. We speak of selection here in the sense that the observer can point out that, from among the many changes he sees as possible, each perturbation has triggered ("chosen") one and not another from that whole body. In point of fact, this description is not wholly adequate, for in each ontogeny there occurs only a number of interactions and there is triggered only a number of structural changes, and the whole body of changes that the observer sees as possible exist only in his mind, even though they are possible for different histories. Under the circumstances, the word "selection" denotes the observer's understanding of what occurs in each ontogeny, even though this understanding arises from his comparative observation of many ontogenies.

There are other expressions we could use to describe this phenomenon. Our purpose in referring to it, however, in terms of a selection of paths of structural change is that the word has become inseparable from the history of biology since the time Darwin used it. In his *Origin of Species*, Darwin pointed up from the first time the relation between generational variation and structural coupling. He stated it was "as if" there were a natural selection, comparable in its separating effect to the artificial selection that a farmer makes of the varieties that interest him. Darwin himself was very clear in pointing out that he never intended to use that word as anything other than an apt metaphor. But soon after, as the theory of evolution began to spread, the notion of "natural selection" came to be interpreted as a source of instructive interactions from the environment. At this point in the history of biology, it would be impossible to change its nomenclature; it is better to use it, but with the proper understanding. Biology, too, has its ontogeny!

environment can be seen as an ongoing "selector" of structural changes that the organism undergoes in its ontogeny.

In a strict sense, the same could be said about environment. Thus we could say that living beings which interact in it operate as selectors of their structural change. For example, the fact that among all the gases possible the cells dispersed oxygen during the first million years after the origin of living beings led to substantial changes in the Earth's atmosphere, so that this gas exists today to a significant degree as a result of that history. Then, too, the presence of oxygen in the atmosphere may have selected structural variations in many lineages of living beings which throughout their phylogeny led to the stabilization of forms that function as oxygen-breathing beings. Structural coupling is always mutual; both organism and environment undergo transformations.

Now, structural coupling between organism and environment takes place between operationally independent systems. If we turn our attention to the maintenance of the organisms as dynamic systems in their environment, this maintenance will appear to us as centered on a compatibility of the organisms with their environment which we call adaptation. If at any time, however, we observe a destructive interaction between a living being and its environment, and the former disintegrates as an autopoietic system, we see the disintegrating living system as having lost its adaptation. The adaptation of a unity to an environment, therefore, is a necessary consequence of that unity's structural coupling with that environment; and this should not be surprising. In other words, every ontogeny as an individual history of structural change is a structural drift that occurs with *conservation of organization and adaptation.*

We say it again: conservation of autopoiesis and conservation of adaptation are necessary conditions for the existence of living beings; the ontogenic structural change of a living being in an environment always occurs as a structural drift congruent with the structural drift of the environment. This drift will appear to an observer as having been "selected" by the environment throughout the history of interactions of the living being, as long as it is alive.

Phylogeny and Evolution

At this point we have all the elements we need to understand the complex history of transformations of living beings during their history. And we can now answer the questions that we raised at the beginning of this chapter. The diligent reader will have realized that in order to delve into this phenomenon, we have examined under a conceptual microscope what occurs in the history of individual interactions. For if we understand how this occurs *in each individual case* and know that there will be variations at each reproductive stage, we can telescope millions of years and see the results of a large (very large!) number of repetitions of the same phenomenon of individual ontogeny followed by reproductive change. Figure 26 gives us an overall view of the history of living beings, from its beginning to our present day, in all its splendor.

This figure resembles a tree, and so it is called the phylogenetic history of species. A phylogeny is a succession of organic forms sequentially gen-

erated by reproductive relationships. The changes experienced throughout the phylogeny constitute phylogenetic or evolutionary change.

For instance, Figure 27 depicts the drift of a particular group of metacellulars, some now-extinct marine invertebrates known as trilobites. With

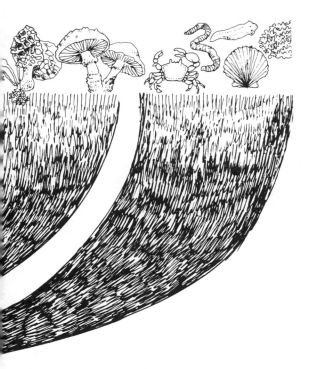

Fig. 26. The great paths of organic evolution, from prokaryotic origins to the present, with the whole variety of unicellulars, plants, animals, and fungi which emerge from the branching and intercrossing by symbiosis of many primordial lineages.

variations at each reproductive stage in the unicellular phase of the animal, a great diversity of types within that group (as we see at each moment in the history of trilobites) was generated. Each one of these variants is coupled to an environment, a variant of one central theme. Over this long sequence, dramatic geologic transformations occurred on the earth, such as those at the end of the so-called Triassic period some 200 million years ago. The fossil record reveals to us that, during this time, most of the lineages of trilobites disappeared. That is to say, the structural variations produced in those lineages did not prove to be complementary to the contemporary structural variations of the environment; consequently, the organisms that constituted those lineages did not

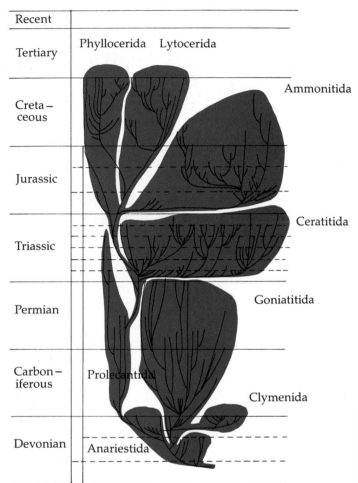

Recent

Tertiary — Phyllocerida   Lytocerida

Creta–ceous

Ammonitida

Jurassic

Triassic

Ceratitida

Permian

Goniatitida

Carbon–iferous — Prolecantida

Clymenida

Devonian — Anariestida

Fig. 27. Expansion and extinction in lineages of a group of trilobites, animals that existed between 300 and 500 million years ago.

conserve their adaptation, did not reproduce, and those lineages were interrupted. The lineages in which this did not occur survived for many more millions of years but, eventually, repeated drastic changes in the environment of the trilobites resulted in the extinction of all their lineages because their members did not conserve adaptation.

A study of fossil remnants and paleontology enables us to reconstruct histories similar to the history of trilobites for each one of the animal and plant types known today. There is not a single case in the structural history of living beings which does not reveal that each lineage is a particular case of variations on a basic theme, over an uninterrupted sequence of reproductive changes with conservation of autopoiesis and adaptation.

Note that this case (like all the other cases) reveals that there are many structural variations capable of producing individuals that can survive in a given environment. All these variations, as we saw before, are equally adapted. They are capable of continuing the lineage to which they belong in their particular environment, whether it is changing or not, at least for some thousands of years. But this case also reveals that the different lineages which the different structural variations bring about in the course of a group's evolutive history, differ in the opportunity they have to maintain uninterrupted their contribution to the group's variety in a changing environment. We see this in a retrospective view: there are lineages that disappear, revealing that the structural configurations that characterized them did not enable them to conserve the organization and adaptation needed for their continuity. In the process of organic evolution, once the essential ontogenic requisite of reproduction is fulfilled, everything is made possible. Reproduction is a necessity; otherwise there is extinction. We shall see later how this conditions significantly the cognitive history of living beings.

Natural Drift

Let us look at this wonderful tree of organic evolution through an analogy. Imagine a hill with a sharp peak. Picture yourself at the top, flicking down drops of water, always in the same direction, even though (because of the mechanics of your action) there are variations in how they begin to fall. Now, imagine that the successive drops are leaving marks on the ground as a record of their fall.

Evidently, if we repeat our experiment many times, we will get slightly different results. Some drops will go straight down; others will meet with obstacles that they will elude in different ways because of their small differences in weight or impetus, going off to one side or the other. The wind may change slightly and move the drops in sinuous ways or away from the initial direction; also, the marks left by previous drops will leave a different surface for subsequent ones, and so on indefinitely.

Let us take this series of experiments and, following the trails left by each drop, let us mark out the paths we have collected, as though the water had been spilled all at once. We shall get something like what is shown in Figure 28.

This figure can adequately represent the many natural drifts of water drops on the hill, a result of different individual ways of interaction with the irregularities of the land, the wind, and so forth. The analogy with living beings is obvious. The peak and the initial direction chosen are equivalent to a common ancestral organism that gives rise to descendants with slight structural changes. The multiple repetition is equivalent to the many lineages that arise from those descendants. The hill, of course, is the entire surrounding environment of the living beings. It changes through history, partly independent of the way living beings develop and partly dependent on them, which we associate here with the diminishing altitude; at the same time, we associate the continuous descent of the water drops, in continuous conservation of the decrease in potential energy, with the conservation of adaptation. In this analogy we have skipped the reproductive stages because what we are representing is the unfoldment of lineages, not how they form.

This analogy does show us, however, that the natural drift will follow only the courses that are possible at each instant, often without any great variation in the appearance of the organisms (phenotype) and often with many ramifications, depending on the kinds of organism-environment relations that are conserved. Organisms and environment vary independently: the organisms at each reproductive stage and the environment according to a different dynamics. From the encounter of these two variations will emerge phenotypic stabilization and diversification as a result of the same process of conservation of adaptation, and autopoiesis depending on when the encounter takes place: stabilization when the environment changes slowly, diversification and extension when it changes abruptly. Constancy and variation of lineages will depend, therefore, on the interplay between the historical conditions under which the organisms live and on their intrinsic properties as individuals. For this reason, in the natural drift of living beings there will be many extinctions, many surprising forms, and all sorts of forms imaginable that we shall never see appear.

Let us imagine now another view of the paths of the natural drift of living beings, looking at those paths from above. The primordial form is now at the center, and the lineages derived from that

Fig. 28. The natural drift of
living beings seen as a metaphor of the water drop.

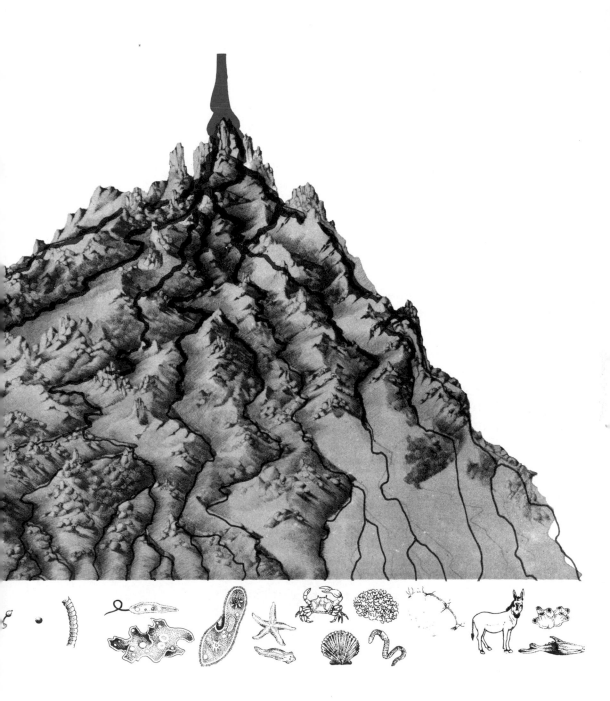

form are distributed all around, like branches that emerge from the center and keep spreading out from it while the organisms involved keep differentiating from the original form.[4] (See Fig. 29.)

Looking at it this way, we see that most lineages of living beings we find today are above all similar to the first autopoietic unities such as bacteria or blue-green algae. All these lineages are equivalent to histories that are close to the central point. Some paths separate, to constitute the variety of multicellular beings. And some separate even more, to constitute higher vertebrates: birds and mammals. As in the case of the water drops, given sufficient cases and sufficient time, many of the lineages possible—as far removed as they appear—are going to occur. In addition, some of the lineages are interrupted because there arrives a time, as we indicated when speaking of trilobites, when the reproductive diversity they generate is not commensurate with environmental variation; and conservation of adaptation dies out, because beings are produced that are incapable of reproduction in their given environment.

In the system of biologic lineages there are many paths that have lasted millions of years with few variations around a fundamental form, many that have given rise to new forms, and, lastly, many that have become extinct without leaving a branch reaching to the present. In all these cases, however, it is a matter of phylogenetic drifts in which are conserved the organization and adaptation of organisms that make up the lineages as long as they exist. Furthermore, it is not the variations in the environment that an observer may see that determine the evolutive path of the different lineages, but the course followed by the conservation of structural coupling of the organisms in

4. Original concept of Raúl Berriós.

Fig. 29. The natural drift of living beings as distances of complexity with respect to their common origin.

their own environment (niche), which they define and whose variations can go unnoticed by an observer. Who can observe the tenuous variations in the force of the wind, the rocks, or the electrostatic charges that can trigger changes in the paths of the water drops depicted in Figure 29? The physicist throws his hands up in despair and speaks merely of random fluctuations. Nevertheless, he knows that under each situation observed there are deterministic processes. That is, he knows that in order to describe what happens with the water drops, he needs a descriptive account, which is practically inaccessible but which he can ignore if he gives a probabilistic description. Such description predicts the class of phenomena that may occur, but no case in particular.

To understand the phenomenon of evolution, the biologist finds himself in a similar situation.

More or Less Well Adapted

We have said that as long as a living being does not disintegrate, it is adapted to its environment and therefore that its condition of adaptation is an invariant, i.e., it is conserved. We have also said that in this sense all living beings are the same while they are alive. We have often heard it said, however, that there are beings more or less adapted, or found to be adapted as a result of their evolutive history.

Like many of the descriptions of biological evolution that we have garnered from schoolbooks, this description of adaptation as a variable (in the light of everything we have said) is inadequate. In the best of cases, the observer can introduce a yardstick of comparison or reference in order to make comparisons and speak of efficiency in the embodiment of a function. For instance, one could measure efficiency of oxygen consumption in different groups of aquatic animals and show that some organisms use less oxygen than others under conditions that seem to entail the same effort. Can we say that those organisms that consume less oxygen are more efficient and better adapted? Certainly not, because as long as they are alive, they have all met the requirements for an uninterrupted ontogeny. Comparisons about efficiency belong to the realm of the observer's descriptions; they are not directly related to what happens in the individual histories of conservation of adaptation.

Fig. 30. Different ways of swimming.

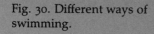

The phenomena that concern him, however, are governed by laws very different from those that govern physical phenomena, as we saw when speaking of the conservation of identity and adaptation. Thus, the biologist can readily account for great lines of evolution in the history of living beings based on their structural coupling to a changing environment (such as the environmental changes we mentioned in the case of trilobites). But he, too, throws up his hands in despair when he tries to explain the detailed transformations of an animal group. To do that, he would have to reconstruct not only all the environmental variations but also the way in which this particular group compensated for those fluctuations according to its own structural plasticity. In short, we are forced to describe each particular case as a resultant of random variations, since we can describe only *a posteriori* how its transformations occurred. In the same way we would observe a

Evolution: Natural Drift

To comprehend this book, it is important to realize that what we said about organic evolution is sufficient for understanding the basic features of the phenomenon of historical transformation of living beings. It is not necessary to scrutinize the underlying mechanisms.

For instance, we have skimmed over what is known today about how population genetics makes explicit some aspects of what Darwin called "modification through descendancy." Likewise, we have not touched upon the contribution made by the study of fossils to a detailed knowledge of the evolutive transformations of many species.

In fact, we have no unified picture of how the evolution of living beings occurs in all its aspects. There are many schools of thought that seriously question understanding evolution by natural selection; this view has prevailed in biology for more than sixty years. Whatever new ideas have been bruited about in terms of evolutive mechanisms, however, those ideas cannot discount the phenomenon of evolution. But they *will* free us from the popular view of evolution as a process in which there is an environmental world to which living beings adapt progressively, optimizing their use of it. What we propose here is that evolution occurs as a phenomenon of structural drift under ongoing phylogenic selection. In that phenomenon there is no progress or optimization of the use of the environment, but only conservation of adaptation and autopoiesis. It is a process in which organism and environment remain in a continuous structural coupling.

drifting boat, moved by changes in wind and waves which we cannot assess.

We can then say that one of the most interesting things about evolution is the way in which the internal coherence of a group of living beings compensates for a particular perturbation. For instance, if there is a significant change in Earth temperature, only those organisms capable of living within new temperature ranges will be able to continue their phylogeny. Compensation for temperature change, however, can come about in many ways: through thick fur, through changes in metabolic rate, through massive geographic migration, and so forth. In each case, what we see as adaptation to the cold also involves the rest of the organism in a *global* way: growing fur, for instance, necessarily implies correlative changes not only in the fur and muscles but also in how animals of the same group recognize each other and the way in which muscle tone is regulated during motion. In other words, since every autopoietic system is a unity of many interdependencies, when one dimension in the system is changed, the whole organism undergoes correlative changes in many dimensions at the same time. But obviously, such correlative changes as seem to us related to changes in the environment do not emerge because of them, but emerge in the structural drift that takes place in the encounters between organism and environment which are operationally independent. As we do not see all the factors involved in this encounter, structural drift seems to be a process that is haphazard. That this is not the case, we shall see when we study the ways in which the coherent whole that makes up an organism undergoes structural changes.

To sum up: evolution is a *natural drift*, a product of the conservation of autopoiesis and adaptation. As in the case of the water drops, there is no need for an outside guiding force to generate diversity and complementarity between organism and environment. Nor is that guiding force needed to explain the directionality of the variations in a lineage, nor is it the case that some specific quality of living beings is being optimized. Evolution is somewhat like a sculptor with wanderlust: he goes through the world collecting a thread here, a hunk of tin there, a piece of wood here, and he combines them in a way that their structure and circumstances allow, with no reason other than what is *able* to combine them. And so, as he wanders about, intricate forms are being produced; they are composed of harmoniously interconnected parts that are a product not of design but of a natural drift. Thus, too, with no law other than the conservation of an identity and the capacity to reproduce, we have all emerged. It is what interconnects us to all things in what is fundamental to us: to the five-petal rose, to the shrimp in the bay, or to the executive in New York City.

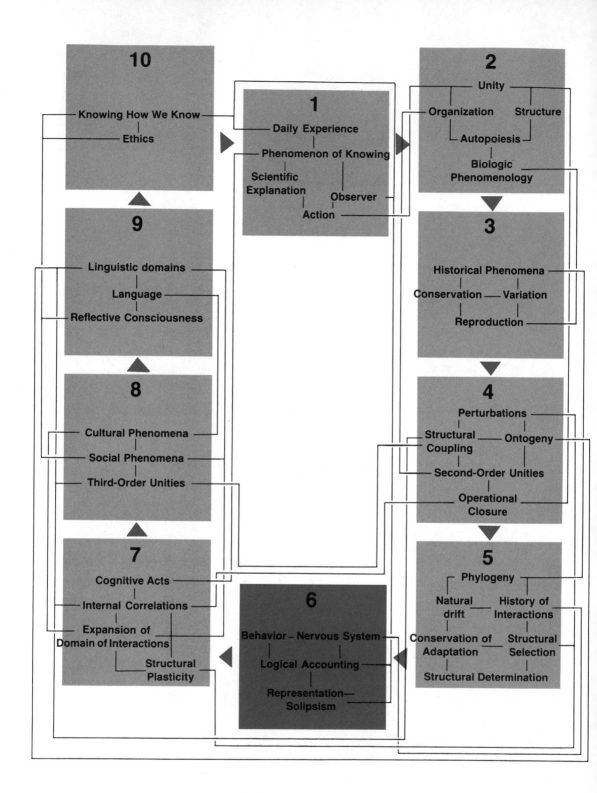

10
Knowing How We Know
Ethics

1
Daily Experience
Phenomenon of Knowing
Scientific
Explanation
Observer
Action

2
Unity
Organization   Structure
Autopoiesis
Biologic
Phenomenology

9
Linguistic domains
Language
Reflective Consciousness

3
Historical Phenomena
Conservation — Variation
Reproduction

8
Cultural Phenomena
Social Phenomena
Third-Order Unities

4
Perturbations
Structural   Ontogeny
Coupling
Second-Order Unities
Operational
Closure

7
Cognitive Acts
Internal Correlations
Expansion of
Domain of Interactions
Structural
Plasticity

6
Behavior — Nervous System
Logical Accounting
Representation—
Solipsism

5
Phylogeny
Natural   History of
drift   Interactions
Conservation of Structural
Adaptation   Selection
Structural Determination

Fig. 31. Orangutan taking a
mouse away from a cat.

When we meet a professional fortune-teller who promises to use his art to reveal our future, we generally have mixed feelings. On the one hand, the idea appeals to us that someone can look into our future by looking at our hands and relying on a determinism that is inscrutable for us but decipherable by him. On the other hand, we resist the idea that we are determined, explainable, and predictable beings. We cherish our free will and want to be beyond determinism. But at the same time, we want the doctor to cure our diseases by treating us as structurally determined systems. What does this tell us? What relation is there between our organic being and our behavior? Our purpose in this chapter and the next ones is to answer these questions. To this end we shall begin by examining more closely how we can understand a behavioral domain in all its possible dimensions.

Predictability and the Nervous System

As we have already seen, we can only come up with a scientific explanation if we treat the phenomenon at hand as a result of the operation of a structurally determined system. Our entire analysis of the world and the living beings that we have presented so far has been done in deterministic terms. Thus seen, the universe becomes comprehensible and living beings emerge in it spontaneously and naturally.

We must now distinguish very clearly between determinism and predictability. We speak of prediction whenever we consider the present state of any system we are observing, then claim that there will be a consequent state in it that will result from its structural dynamics and that we will be able to observe. A prediction, therefore, reveals what we as observers expect to happen.

From this it follows that predictability is not always possible and that it is not the same thing to affirm the structurally determined nature of a system and to affirm its complete predictability. This is so because we may not be in a position as observers to know what we need to know about the operation of a certain system for us to make a predictive statement. Thus, no one disputes that the clouds and the wind blindly obey certain simple principles of movement and transformation. Because it is hard to know all the variables involved, however, meteorology today is only a partially predictive science. In this case our predictive limitation is due to our incapacity to make a thorough observation. In other cases our incapacity is of a different nature. Thus, there are phenomena such as turbulence for which we do not even have elements to help us imagine a detailed deterministic system that would cause it. In this case, our predictive limitation reveals our conceptual limitation. Lastly, there are systems that change their state when under observation; the mere attempt by an observer to predict their structural course removes them from the realm of his predictions.

In other words, what appears to us as necessary and inevitable reveals us to be observers capable of making a valid prediction. What we see as haphazard reveals us to be observers incapable of applying to it a scientific explanation.

To keep these conditions in mind is important especially when we study what happens in the ontogeny of those multicellular organisms with a nervous system, which we regard as endowed with a vast and rich behavioral domain. And this is so because even before we explain what we

mean by a nervous system, we can be sure that
this system, as part of an organism, will have to
function in it by contributing to its structural determination from moment to moment. This contribution will be due both to its very structure and
to the fact that the result of its operation (e.g., language) forms part of the environment which,
from instant to instant, will operate as a selector
in the structural drift of the organism with conservation of adaptation. Living beings (with or
without a nervous system), therefore, function always in their structural present. The past as a reference to interactions gone by and the future as a
reference to interactions yet to come are valuable
dimensions for us to communicate with each other
as observers; however, they do not operate in the
structural determinism of the organism at every
moment.

   With or without a nervous system, all organisms
(ourselves included) function as they function and
are where they are at each instant, because of their
structural coupling. We are writing these words
because we are made in a certain way and we have
gone through a particular ontogeny. The reader as
he reads this understands what he understands
because his structure in the present and, indi-
rectly, his history so determine. Strictly speaking,
nothing is an accident. Our experience, however,
is one of creative freedom; and in the way we see
things, the behavior of higher animals seems un-
predictable. How does this great richness and diversity come about in the behavior of animals with
a nervous system? To understand this question
better, we must closely examine the very operation of the nervous system with all the richness of
the realms of structural coupling that its presence
makes possible.

On Frogs and Wolf Children

All varieties of frogs and toads feed on small animals such as worms, flies, ants, and moths. Their feeding behavior is always similar: the animal orients itself to the prey, unleashes its long, sticky tongue, and retracts it quickly into the mouth, along with the adhering prey. In this the frog's behavior is very effective. The observer notes that it always shoots out its tongue in the direction of the prey.

With an animal like the frog, however, it is possible to do a very revealing experiment. We can take a tadpole, or frog's larva, and, with the careful hand of a surgeon, cut the edge of the eye—respecting its optic nerve—and rotate it 180 degrees. The animal thus operated is left to complete its larval development and metamorphosis until it becomes an adult. Now we do our frog experiment. We cover its rotated eye and show it a worm. The tongue goes out, and we see that it makes a perfect hit. We repeat the experiment, but this time cover the normal eye. In this case we see that the frog shoots out its tongue with a deviation of exactly 180 degrees. That is, if the prey is below and in front of the animal, the frog will now shoot out its tongue backward and up. Each time we repeat the test, it makes the same mistake: a deviation of 180 degrees; there's no point in going on. The animal with the rotated eye will never change its way of shooting out its tongue with a deviation in aim equal to the rotation imposed by the experimenter (Fig. 32). The frog shoots out its tongue as if the retinal zone where the image of the prey is formed were in its normal position.

This experiment reveals in a very dramatic way that, for the animal, there is no such thing as up and down, front and back, in reference to an outside world, as it exists for the observer doing the

study. There is only an *internal correlation* between the place where the retina receives a given perturbation and the muscular contractions that move the tongue, the mouth, the neck, and, in fact, the frog's entire body.

Fig. 32. Is this an error in targeting or an expression of a new internal correlation?

In an animal with a rotated eye, if we place the prey down and forward, we cause a visual perturbation to fall upward and back, in the zone of the retina which is normally down and in front. For the frog's nervous system this triggers a sensory-motor correlation between the position of the retina and the movement of the tongue, and not a computation on a world map as would appear reasonable to the observer.

This experiment,[5] like many others done since the 1950s, can be direct evidence that the operation of the nervous system is an expression of its connectivity or structure of connections and that behavior arises because of the nervous system's *internal* relations of activity. We shall dwell on this later. Right now we wish to call our reader's atten-

5. R. W. Sperry, *Journal of Neurophysiology* 8(1945):15.

tion to the dimension of structural plasticity that the presence of the nervous system introduces into the organism; that is, we shall show how, for each organism, its history of interactions is a history of structural changes that forms a particular history of transformations of an initial structure in which the nervous system participates by expanding the realm of possible states.

If we separate a newborn lamb from its mother for a few hours and return it to her, the lamb will develop in an apparently normal way. The lamb will grow, walk, and follow its mother, and it reveals nothing peculiar until we observe its interactions with other lambs. These animals like to run and play, bumping each other with their heads. The lamb that we separated from its mother for a few hours does not do so. It does not know how and it does not learn how to play. It stays by itself. What happened? We have no detailed answer to this question; however, we know in the light of what we have seen up to now that the dynamics of states of the nervous system depend on its structure. In addition, we know that the fact that this animal behaves in a different way reveals that its nervous system is different from that of the others as a result of the temporary maternal deprivation. In fact, during the first hours after a lamb is born, its mother licks it continually all over its body. In separating the newborn lamb from its mother, we have interfered with this interaction and all it entails in terms of tactile and visual stimulation and, probably, different types of chemical contacts. The experiment shows these interactions to be decisive for a structural transformation of the nervous system which has consequences apparently very remote from the simple behavior of licking.

Every living being comes into existence with a special single cell that constitutes its starting point. For this reason the ontogeny of every living being consists in its ongoing structural transformation. It is a process that, on the one hand, occurs without interruption of class identity and structural coupling between living system and environment from its beginning to its final disintegration; on the other hand, this ontogeny follows a particular course contingent on the sequence of structural changes that its interactions trigger in it. What we said about the lamb, therefore, is no exception. As in the example of the frog, this case seems very evident to us because we have access to a series of interactions that we can describe as "selectors" of a certain path of structural change, which in the case at hand proved to be pathological when compared with the normal course.

That the foregoing applies also to human beings was shown by the dramatic case of two Hindu girls who were rescued (or snatched) in 1922 from a family of wolves with which they lived in the north of India.[6] They had been reared in complete isolation from all human contact (Fig. 33). One of the girls was eight years old and the other five. The younger one died a short time after being found; the other survived another ten years in the company of other orphans with whom she was brought up. At the time they were found, the girls did not know how to walk on two feet. They moved about rapidly on all fours. Of course, they did not speak and had inexpressive faces. They wanted only raw meat and exhibited nocturnal habits. They rejected human contact and preferred the company of dogs or wolves. At the time they were found, they were in perfect health and showed no

6. C. MacLean, *The Wolf Children* (New York: Penguin Books, 1977).

signs of mental retardation or malnutrition. Their separation from the wolf family caused a profound depression in them and brought them to the brink of death.

The girl who survived for ten years eventually changed her dieting habits and her cycles of activity. She learned to walk on two feet, although she would go back to running on four feet under the stress of urgency. She never learned to speak properly, although she did use a few words. The family of the Anglican missionary who looked after her, as also the other persons who came to know her closely, never felt that she was completely human.

This case—and it is not the only one—shows us that although they were human in their genetic constitution and in their anatomy and physiology, these two girls never managed to fit in with a human context. The behavior that the missionary and his family wanted to change in them, because it was unacceptable in a human context, was completely natural to their wolflike upbringing. In fact, Mowgli, the jungle boy of the forest that Kipling imagined, could never have existed in flesh and blood, for he knew how to talk and behaved like a person from the very first moment he encountered a human environment. We who are flesh-and-blood people are no strangers to the world in which we live and which we bring forth through our living.

On the Razor's Edge

The most popular and current view of the nervous system considers it an instrument whereby the organism gets information from the environment which it then uses to build a *representation* of

Fig. 33. (a) and (b) Comparison showing wolflike gait of the Bengali girl sometime after she was found. (c) Wolf girl eating in the way she had learned. (d) She was never felt to be completely human.

a

b

c

d

the world that it uses to compute behavior adequate for its survival in the world (Fig. 34). This view requires that the environment imprint in the nervous system the characteristics proper to it and that the nervous system use them to generate behavior, much the same as we use a map to plot a route.

We know, however, that the nervous system as part of an organism operates with structural determination. Therefore, the structure of the environment cannot specify its changes, but can only trigger them. We as observers have access both to the nervous system and to the structure of its environment. We can thus describe the behav-

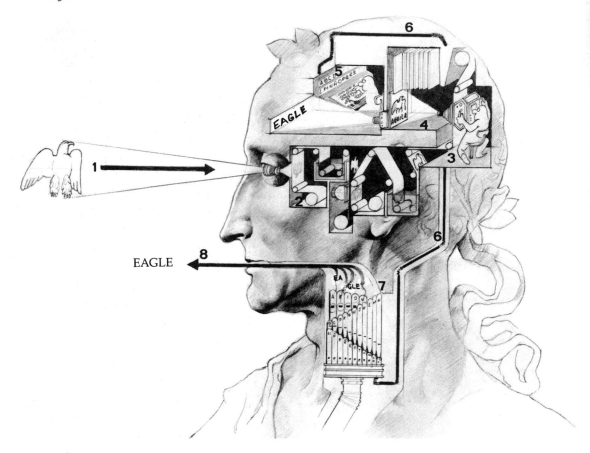

ior of an organism as though it arose from the operation of its nervous system with representations of the environment or as an expression of some goal-oriented process. These descriptions, however, do not reflect the operation of the nervous system itself. They are good only for the purpose of communication among ourselves as observers. They are inadequate for a scientific explanation.

If we reflect a moment on the examples given earlier, we will realize that our first tendency to describe what happens in each case centers, in one way or another, on the use of some form of

Fig. 34. Caesar according to the representationist metaphor.

the metaphor of "getting information" from the
environment represented "within." Our course of
reasoning, however, has made it clear that to use
this type of metaphor contradicts everything we
know about living beings. We are faced with a
formidable snag because it seems that the only
alternative to a view of the nervous system as
operating with representations is to deny the surrounding reality. Indeed, if the nervous system
does not operate—and cannot operate—with a
representation of the surrounding world, what
brings about the extraordinary functional effectiveness of man and animal and their enormous
capacity to learn and manipulate the world? If we
deny the objectivity of a knowable world, are
we not in the chaos of total arbitrariness because
everything is possible?

This is like walking on the razor's edge. On one
side there is a trap: the impossibility of understanding cognitive phenomena if we assume a
world of objects that informs us because there is
no mechanism that makes that "information" possible. On the other side, there is another trap: the
chaos and arbitrariness of nonobjectivity, where
everything seems possible. We must learn to take
the middle road, right on the razor's edge (Fig. 35).

In fact, on the one hand there is the trap of as-
suming that the nervous system operates with
representations of the world. And it *is* a trap, because it blinds us to the possibility of realizing
how the nervous system functions from moment
to moment as a definite system with operational
closure. We shall see this in the next chapter.

On the other hand, there is the other trap: deny-
ing the surrounding environment on the assumption that the nervous system functions completely
in a vacuum, where everything is valid and every-

thing is possible. This is the other extreme: absolute cognitive solitude or solipsism, the classic
philosophic tradition which held that only one's
interior life exists. And it is a trap because it does
not allow us to explain how there is a due propor-
tion or commensurability between the operation
of the organism and its world.

Now, these two extremes or traps have existed
from the very first attempts to understand cognition, even in its most classical roots. Today, the
representational extreme prevails; at other times
the opposing view prevailed.

Fig. 35. The epistemologic
Odyssey: sailing between the
Scylla monster of representa-
tionism and the Charybdis
whirlpool of solipsism.

We wish to propose now a way to cut this apparent Gordian knot and find a natural way to avoid the two abysses of the razor's edge. By now the attentive reader has surmised what we are going to say because it is contained in what we said before. The solution is to maintain a clear *logical accounting*. It means never losing sight of what we stated at the beginning: everything said is said by someone. The solution, like all solutions to apparent contradictions, lies in moving away from the opposition and changing the nature of the question, to embrace a broader context.

The situation is actually simple. As observers we can see a unity in *different* domains, depending on the distinctions we make. Thus, on the one hand, we can consider a system in that domain where its components operate, in the domain of its internal states and its structural changes. Thus considered, for the internal dynamics of the system, the environment does not exist; it is irrelevant. On the other hand, we can consider a unity that also interacts with its environment and describes its history of interactions with it. From this perspective in which the observer can establish relations between certain features of the environment and the behavior of the unity, the internal dynamics of that unity are irrelevant.

Neither of these two possible descriptions is a problem per se: both are necessary to complete our understanding of a unity. It is the observer who correlates them from his outside perspective. It is he who recognizes that the structure of the system determines its interactions by specifying which configurations of the environment can trigger structural changes in it. It is he who recognizes that the environment does not specify or direct the structural changes of a system. The problem begins when we unknowingly go from one realm to the other and demand that the correspondences we establish between them (because we see these two realms simultaneously) be in fact a part of the operation of the unity—in this case, the organism and nervous system. If we are able to keep our logical accounting in order, this complication vanishes; we become aware of these two perspectives and relate them in a broader realm that we establish. In this way we do not need to fall back on representations or deny that the system operates in an environment that is familiar owing to its history of structural coupling.

Perhaps an analogy will clarify this. Imagine a person who has always lived in a submarine. He has never left it and has been trained how to handle it. Now, we are standing on the shore and see the submarine gracefully surfacing. We then get on the radio and tell the navigator inside: "Congratulations! You avoided the reefs and surfaced beautifully. You really know how to handle a submarine." The navigator in the submarine, however, is perplexed: "What's this about reefs and surfacing? All I did was push some levers and turn knobs and make certain relationships between indicators as I operated the levers and

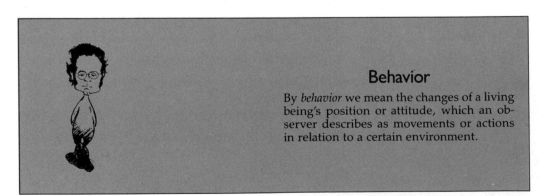

Behavior

By *behavior* we mean the changes of a living being's position or attitude, which an observer describes as movements or actions in relation to a certain environment.

knobs. It was all done in a prescribed sequence which I'm used to. I didn't do any special maneuver, and on top of that, you talk to me about a submarine. You must be kidding!"

All that exists for the man inside the submarine are indicator readings, their transitions, and ways of obtaining specific relations between them. It is only for us on the outside, who see how relations change between the submarine and its environment, that the submarine's behavior exists and that it appears more or less adequate according to the consequences involved. If we are to maintain logical accounting, we must not confuse the operation of the submarine itself and its dynamics of different states with its movements and changing positions in the environment. The dynamics of the submarine's different states, with its navigator who does not know the outside world, never occurs in an operation with representations of the world that the outside observer sees: it involves neither "beaches" nor "reefs" nor "surface" but only correlations between indicators within certain limits. Entities such as beaches, reefs, or surface are valid only for an outside observer, not for the submarine or for the navigator who functions as a component of it.

What is valid for the submarine in this analogy is valid also for all living systems: for the frog with the rotated eye, for the wolf girl, and for each one of us human beings.

Behavior and the Nervous System

What we call behavior in observing the changes of state of an organism in its environment corresponds to the description we make of the movements of the organism in an environment that we indicate. Behavior is not something that the living being *does* in itself (for in it there are only internal structural changes) but something that we point to. Inasmuch as the changes of state of an organism (with or without a nervous system) depend on its structure and this structure depends on its history of structural coupling, changes of state of the organism in its environment will necessarily be suitable and familiar to it, independently of the behavior or environment we are describing. For this reason, if a behavior as a particular configuration of movements is to appear adequate, it will depend on the environment in which we describe it. The success or failure of a behavior is always defined by the expectations that the observer specifies. If the reader were in the desert and did the same movements and postures that he now adopts in reading this book, his behavior would not only be eccentric but pathologic.

Thus, the behavior of living beings is not an invention of the nervous system and it is not exclusively associated with it, for the observer will see behavior when he looks at any living being in its environment. What the nervous system does is *expand* the realm of possible behaviors by endowing the organism with a tremendously versatile and plastic structure. This is the topic of the next chapter.

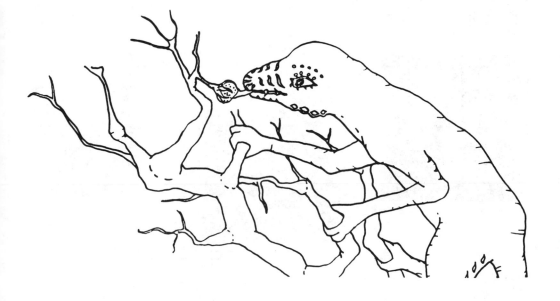

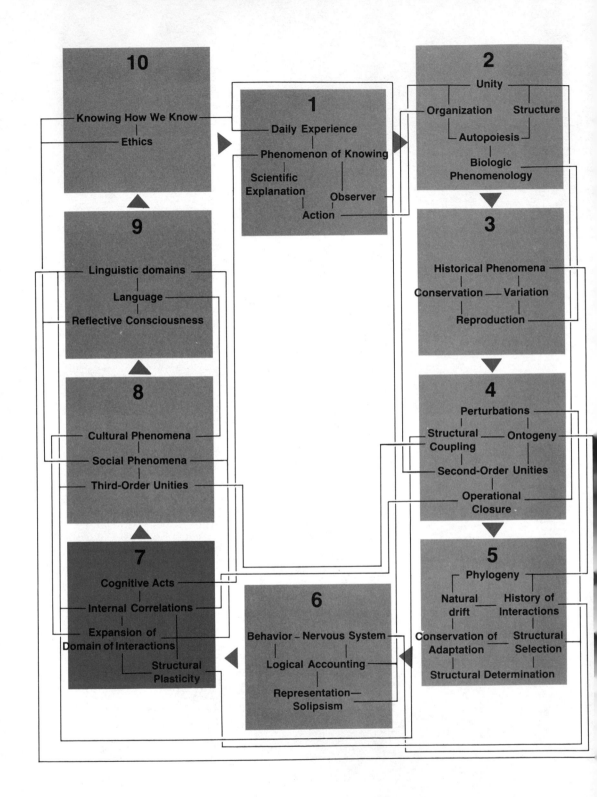

7 The Nervous System and Cognition

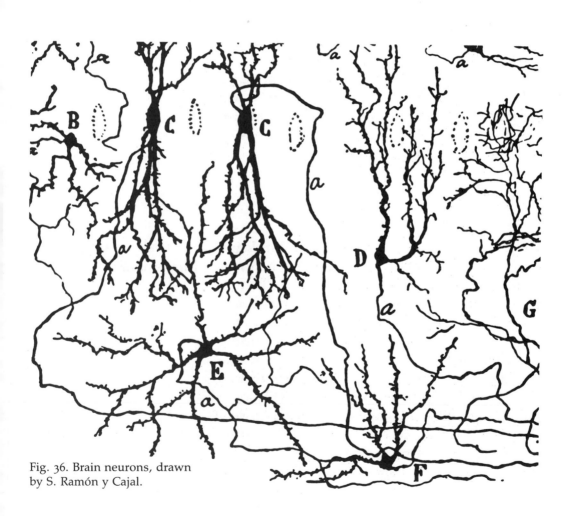

Fig. 36. Brain neurons, drawn by S. Ramón y Cajal.

In this chapter we wish to examine *in what way* the nervous system expands the realms of interaction of an organism. We have already seen that behavior is not an invention of the nervous system. It is proper to any unity seen in an environment where the unity specifies a realm of perturbations and maintains its organization owing to the changes of state that these perturbations trigger in it.

We must keep this clearly in mind, for we usually regard behavior as something proper to animals with a nervous system. Moreover, the usual associations with the word "behavior" come from actions such as walking, eating, searching, and so forth. If we examine closely what is common to all these activities currently associated with the notion of behavior, we find they all have to do with *movement*. But movement, whether on land or in water, is not universal to living beings. Among the many forms resulting from natural drift, there are many that show no movement.

Natural History of Movement

Let us consider, for example, the plant in Figure 37. When this sagittaria grows outside the water, it has the form illustrated at the top. When the water level rises, however, and the plant is submerged, it changes structure in a few days and transforms into its aquatic form, shown at the bottom of the illustration. The situation is reversible; it occurs with structural transformations that are quite complex and that have to do with a certain form of differentiation in the several parts of the plant. This is a case we could describe as behavior, for there are structural changes that appear as observable changes in the plant's form to compensate for recurrent disturbances of the en-

Fig. 37. *Sagittaria sagitufolia* in its aquatic and terrestrial forms.

vironment. This situation, however, is normally described as a change in the plant's development and not in its behavior. Why?

Let us compare the case of the sagittaria with the feeding behavior of an amoeba about to ingest a small protozoan by extending its pseudopods (Fig. 38). These pseudopods are protoplasm expansions or digitations that can be associated with changes in the local physicochemical makeup of the cell membrane and matrix. The result is that the protoplasm flows at certain points and pushes the animal in one direction or another, which results in its amoeboid movements. In contrast to what happens with the sagittaria, no one hesitates to describe this situation as behavior.

From our standpoint, it is clear that between both cases there is a continuity. Both are instances of behavior. It is interesting to note that it is easier for us to call one—and not the other—a case of behavior, only because we can detect movement in the amoeba and not in the sagittaria. That is, there is a continuity between this movement in the amoeba and the great diversity of behaviors of higher animals which we always see as forms of movement. By contrast, the changes in differ-

Fig. 38. Ingestion.

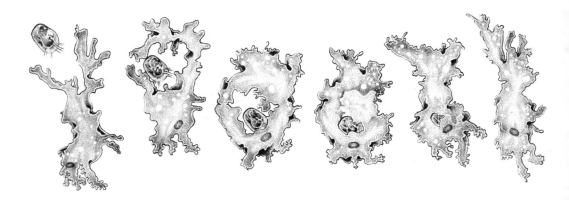

Fig. 39. Relations of size and speed in nature.

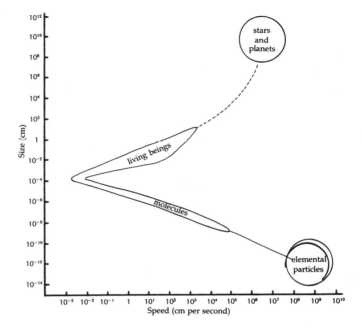

entiation of the sagittaria seem remote from what we know as movement because of their slowness, and we see it only as a change in form. Actually, from the standpoint of the nervous system's appearance and transformation, the possibility of movement is essential. This is what makes the history of movement so fascinating. Exactly how and why are what we are going to see throughout this chapter. But first let us look at general cases from a wider perspective. We shall now consider movement as it appears in varied realms of nature.

Figure 39 shows the size of different natural unities in terms of their capacity to move, as measured with respect to maximum speed.[7] Thus, it is evident that regarding the extremes of big and small, both the galaxies and the elemental particles are capable of very fast movement in the order of thousands of miles per second. If we consider large molecules as those which con-

7. J. T. Bonner, *The Evolution of Culture in Animal Societies* (Princeton, N.J.: Princeton University Press, 1980).

stitute living beings, their movement becomes slower as their size becomes bigger and they move in viscous surroundings formed by other molecules. Thus, there are molecules that contain many of the proteins of our organization which are so large that their spontaneous movement is insignificant when compared with the mobility of smaller molecules.

It is under these circumstances that (as we saw in Chapter 2) autopoietic systems appear; this is made possible by the existence of these many large organic molecules. Once the much larger molecules formed, the curve shows a brisk shift in which the history of cell transformations led to the origin of structures such as flagella or pseudopods, which again allow for considerable movement, because they call into play forces much greater than those of viscosity. Moreover, when multicellular organisms originate, some of them develop—through cell differentiation— much more spectacular locomotive capacities. Thus, an impala can run at a speed of many miles an hour, even though it is many times bigger in size than a small molecule that moves (on the average) at the same speed. Metazoa and motile single-cell organisms therefore create a range of movement which, for their size, is unique in nature.

Let us not lose sight, however, of the fact that the appearance of this type of movement is neither universal nor necessary for all forms of living beings. Plants are a fundamental case resulting from a natural drift in which movement is essentially absent as a way of being. Presumably, this is related to the fact that plants are maintained through photosynthesis under the following conditions: they have a constant local supply of nutrients and water from the ground, and gases and light from the atmosphere. This allows conservation of adaptation without the need for large or rapid movements during most of the plant's ontogeny.

To an observer, it is evident that movement poses many possibilities. Many of them are embodied in living beings as a result of their natural drift. Thus, motile organisms base not only their reproduction on movement but also their feeding and modes of interaction with the environment. It is in relation to these living beings in whom natural drift has led to the establishing of motility that the nervous system becomes important. This is what we shall look at now in greater detail.

Sensorimotor Coordination in Single-Cell Organisms

Let us return for a moment to the amoeba at the point of engulfing a protozoan. What is happening in this sequence? It can be summed up in this way: the presence of the protozoan generates a concentration of substances in the environment. These substances are capable of interacting with the amoeba membrane, triggering changes in the consistency of the protoplasm which result in the formation of a pseudopod. The pseudopod, in turn, causes changes in the position of the moving animal, thus modifying the number of molecules in the environment which interact with its membrane. This cycle is repeated, and the sequence of movements of the amoeba is therefore produced through the maintenance of an *internal correlation* between the degree of change of its membrane and those protoplasmic changes we see as pseudopods. That is, a recurrent or invariable correlation is established between a perturbed or sensory surface of the organism and an area capable of

producing movement (motor surface), which
maintains unchanged a set of internal relations in
the amoeba.

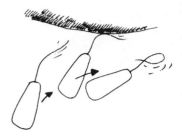

Another example can help clarify this idea. Figure 40 shows a protozoan that has a special structure called a flagellum. This flagellum beats in
such a way that it is capable of moving the protozoan in its fluid medium or environment. In this
particular case, the flagellum beats so that it pulls
the cell behind it. In this swimming action, at
times the protozoan hits an obstacle. What occurs
in that situation? There is an interesting behavior
in relation to change of orientation: the flagellum
bends as it hits the obstacle. This bending triggers
changes in the flagellum's base that is embedded
in the cell. This cell, in turn, triggers changes in
the cytoplasm that slightly rotate it, so that when
the beating begins again, it moves the cell in a
different direction. As a result, the protozoan
touches the obstacle, bends, then avoids it. Again,
as in the case of the amoeba, what is happening
here is that a certain internal correlation is being
maintained between a structure capable of admit-
ting certain perturbations (sensory surface) and a
structure capable of generating movement (motor
surface). The interesting thing about this example
is that both the sensory surface and the motor
surface are the *same;* therefore, their coupling is
immediate.

Fig. 40. Sensorimotor correlation in a swimming
protozoan.

Let us consider another example of this coupling between sensory surfaces and motor surfaces.
There are single-cell bacteria that have flagella
similar in appearance to those of some protozoa.
As Figure 41 shows, however, these flagella function very differently.[8] Instead of beating as in the
other case, they simply remain fixed on their base
and rotate, so that they are like a propeller for the

8. H. Berg, *Scientific American*
233(1975):36.

Fig. 41. Flagellar propulsion in bacteria.

bacteria. Moreover, both directions are possible in these rotations. But there is one direction in which the coordination of the rotations results in a clear-cut movement of the bacteria, whereas in the opposite direction of rotation the coordination causes the bacteria simply to tumble about in the same place. It is possible to follow the movements of one of these bacteria under the microscope and see its changes, under different controlled conditions. If the bacterium is placed, for instance, in an environment where a grain of sugar has been put in one corner, we note that the bacterium stops its tumbling behavior, changes the direction of rotation of the flagella, and heads for the zone of greatest sugar concentration following the path of its gradient of concentration. How does this occur? It happens that in the membrane of the bacterium there are special molecules capable of interacting with the sugar, so that as there is a difference of concentration in a small area around the bacterium, changes take place within it; these changes make the flagellum rotate in a different direction. At each moment, therefore, a stable correlation is again established between the sensory surface and the motor surface of the cell, which gives it a clearly discriminatory behavior as it heads for the zones of greater concentration of certain substances. This is known as chemotaxis. It is an example of behavior on a single-cell level, many of whose molecular details are known.

Unlike these bacteria, the sagittaria which we mentioned, and other plants, do not have a motor surface that endows them with movement. In fact, we find among bacteria some cases that are a sort of compromise between capacity to move and incapacity to move. For instance, when *Caulobacter* is in a very humid environment, it remains fixed to the ground by a plantlike pedestal. During a period of dehydration, however, the bacteria reproduce and new cells grow with a flagellum capable of transporting them to a more humid environment.

We have seen in the foregoing examples that movement (behavior) in single-cell organisms is based on a very specific correlation between their sensory surfaces and their motor surfaces responsible for movement. We have also seen that this correlation occurs through processes inside the cell, that is, through metabolic transformations proper to the cell unity. What happens in the case of metacellular organisms?

Multicellular Sensorimotor Correlation

Let us examine this situation, again through an example. Figure 42 shows a photograph of a hydra, which resembles those found in many ponds. These metazoa belong to a group of coelenterates, an ancient lineage of animals made up of a double layer of cells in the form of a vase. Tentacles at its edge permit it to move in the water and capture other animals, which it takes in and digests by secreting digestive fluids. If we look at the cell structure of this animal, we see a double layer: one facing inside and the other outside. One of these two surfaces seems to have a certain cell diversity. Thus, there are cells with little darts. On being touched, these cells shoot out their projectiles. Other cells possess vacuoles capable of secreting digestive liquids on the inside. We also find in the hydra some motor cells that possess contractile fibers, positioned longitudinally and radially on the wall of the animal (Fig. 43). When

Fig. 42. A small coelenterate:
the hydra.

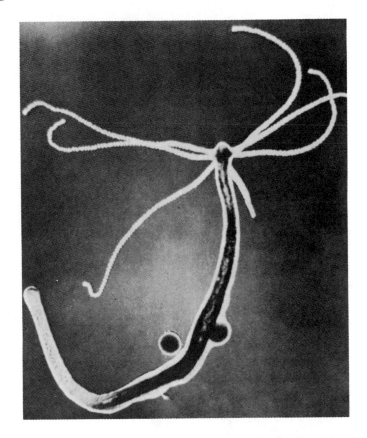

these muscle cells contract in varied combinations,
they cause the animal to move in different ways.

To produce a coordinated action between, say,
the muscle cells of the tentacles and the secretory
cells on the inside, evidently there must be some
type of coupling between these cells. It is not
enough for them to be simply arranged in a double
layer.

To understand how this coupling takes place,
we have to look more carefully at what exists between both cell layers. There we find a peculiar
type of cell, with prolongations that extend for a
considerable length within the animal. These cells

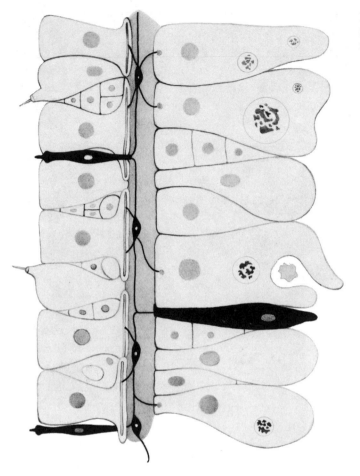

Fig. 43. Sketch of cell diversity in tissues of the hydra, with neurons highlighted.

are peculiar in that, through their prolongations, they establish contact with topographically distant cellular elements of a metozoan. These cells are nervous cells or neurons in their most simple and primitive form. The hydra has one of the simplest forms of nervous system known. It is made up of a network that includes these particular cells, as also receptors and effectors. On the whole, the hydra's nervous system is like a maze of interconnections that extends to all parts of the animal through the space between the cells. In this way, it causes an interaction of the sensory and motor elements that are distant.

Thus we have, complete in all its details, the same situation we had in the case of single-cell behavior: a sensory surface (in this case, sensory cells), a motor surface (in this case, muscle and secretory cells), and a system of coordination between both surfaces (the neuronal network). And the hydra's behavior (feeding, flight, reproduction, etc.) results from the different ways in which these two surfaces (sensory and motor) are dynamically related, via the intraneuronal network, to constitute the nervous system.

Neuronal Structure

What distinguishes neurons is their cytoplasmatic ramifications in specific forms which extend for enormous distances, reaching tens of millimeters in the largest ones. This universal neuronal characteristic, present in all organisms with a nervous system, determines the specific way in which the nervous system participates in the second-order unities that it integrates by placing in contact cellular elements located in different parts of the body. We cannot disregard all the exquisite transformations required for the growth of a cell initially measuring a few millionths of a millimeter into specific forms with ramifications that can reach tens of millimeters in an expansion of several orders of magnitude (Fig. 44).

It is therefore through their physical presence that neurons couple, in many different ways, cellular groups which otherwise could be coupled only through the general circulation of internal substances of the organism. The physical presence of a neuron enables substances to be transported between two regions through a very specific path that does not affect the surrounding cells and their local delivery. The particular feature of connections and interactions that the neuronal forms make possible is the master key to the operation of the nervous system.

There are many types of reciprocal influences between neurons. Best known of all is an electrical discharge that propagates along the neuronal prolongation called the axon, at a wildfire speed. That is why the nervous system is often said to be an organ that functions on the basis of electrical exchanges. This is only partially true,

however, for neurons interact not only through electrical exchanges but also and in a constant way through substances which are transported inside the axon and which, released (or picked up) at the terminals, trigger in the neurons, in the effectors or in the sensors to which they are connected, changes in differentiation and growth.

With what types of cells do neurons connect? Actually, they connect with almost all cell types within an organism; however, they connect, with their expansions, mostly with other neurons. These nervous expansions are, in turn, very specialized; they are known as dendrites and axon

Fig. 44. The neuron and its extension.

Synapse

A *synapse* is a point of close contact between neuron and neuron, or between neurons and other cells, as in a neuromuscular synapse. At these points, the membranes of both cells are closely attached to each other. Moreover, at these points the membranes are specialized and secrete special molecules, namely, neurotransmitters. For this reason, a nervous impulse that goes through a neuron and arrives at a synaptic ending produces secretion in the neurotransmitter which crosses the space between the membranes and triggers an electric exchange in the receiving cell. It is only through specializations like these that a localized mutual influence—and not a diffuse or generalized one, as would occur if interactions were through changes in concentration of some molecules in the bloodstream—is possible between neurons, as also between neurons and other cells.

On each neuron, in its dendritic tree, there are many thousands of synaptic endings from many hundreds of different neurons. Each one of the endings will make a small contribution to the total exchange of electric activity of the neuron to which it is connected. In addition, each neuron is capable of chemically influencing the structure of all the neurons connected to it

(Fig. 45) through the diffusion of metabolites that go out and penetrate along the synaptic surfaces, and go up along the axons or dendrites to the respective cell bodies. On this double metabolic electric traffic depends, at each moment, the state of activity as well as the structural state of each neuron in the nervous system.

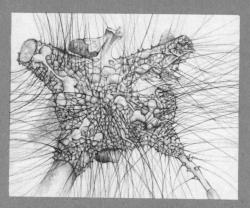

Fig. 45. Three-dimensional reconstruction of all the synaptic contacts that the cell body receives from a motoneuron of the spinal medulla.

terminals. Both in these zones and in the cell bodies, contacts called synapses are established. A synapse is the point where mutual influences are effectively produced between a neuron and that with which it makes contact. Synapses, therefore, are the effective structures that enable the nervous system to carry reciprocal influences between distant cell groups.

Although the overwhelming majority of synaptic contacts in the nervous system are between neurons, these neurons form synapses with many other cell types in the organism. Such is the case of the cells that we have been calling collectively the sensory surface. In the hydra, for instance, this would include all the cells capable of responding to specific perturbations, either of the environment (such as the spearlike cells) or of the organism itself (such as chemoreceptor cells). Likewise, there are neurons that connect with cells of the motor surface, especially the muscles, in a very precise pattern. In short, the neuronal system is embedded in the organism through many contacts with varied cellular classes, operating as a network of precise neuronal interactions together with the cells of the sensory and motor surfaces.

The Interneuronal Network

This basic architecture of the nervous system is universal and valid not only for the hydra, but also for higher vertebrates, including human beings. The sole difference lies not in the fundamental organization of the network that generates sensorimotor correlations, but in the form in which this network is embodied through neurons and connections that vary from one animal species to the other. Indeed, a survey of the neuronal types found in the nervous systems of animals shows an enormous diversity. Some of these neuronal varieties are shown in Figure 46. Moreover, if we keep in mind that the human brain has more than 10^{10} and perhaps more than 10^{11} neurons (tens of billions) and that each one of them receives many contacts with other neurons and connects, in turn, with many cells, the combinations of possible interactions are more than astronomical.

But we emphasize: the basic organization of this immensely complicated human nervous system follows essentially the same logic as in the humble hydra. In the series of transformations of lineages that go from the hydra to mammals, we meet with designs that are variations on the same theme. In worms, for instance, the nervous tissue understood as a network of neurons has been separated like a compartment inside the animal, with nerves along which pass connections that come and go from the sensory surfaces and motor surfaces.

Fig. 46. Neuronal diversity: (*left to right*) bipolar cell of the retina, cell body of a motoneuron of the spinal medulla, mitral cell of the olfactory bulb, pyramidal cell of the cerebral cortex of a mammal.

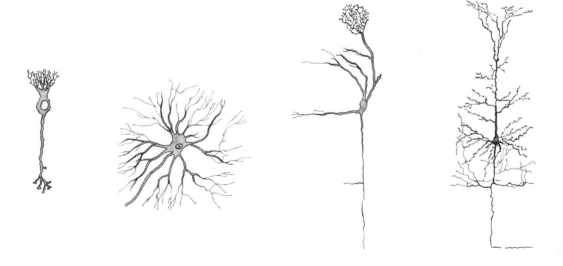

Each variation in the animal's motor state will become the product of a certain pattern of activity in certain groups of neurons connected to the muscles (motoneurons). This motor activity, however, generates many changes in the sensory cells located in the muscles, in other parts of the body, and on the surface of contact with the environment, as also in the motoneurons. This occurs in a process brought about by means of changes in the network of interposed neurons, or interneurons, which interconnects them. In this way there is a continuous sensorimotor correlation determined and mediated by the pattern of activity of this interneuronal network. Since there can be a practically unlimited number of possible states within this network, the possible behaviors of the organism can also be practically unlimited.

This is the key mechanism whereby the nervous system expands the realm of interactions of an organism: *it couples the sensory and motor surfaces through a network of neurons whose pattern can be quite varied.* The mechanism is eminently simple. Once established, however, it permits many different realms of behavior in the phylogeny of metazoa. In fact, the nervous systems of varied species essentially differ only in the specific patterns of their interneuronal networks.

Thus, in humans, some 10^{11} (one hundred billion) interneurons interconnect some 10^6 (one million) motoneurons that activate a few thousand muscles, with some 10^7 (ten million) sensory cells distributed as receptor surfaces throughout the body. Between motor and sensory neurons lies the brain, like a gigantic mass of interneurons that interconnects them (at a ratio 10:100,000:1) in an everchanging dynamics.

For example, Fig. 47 shows a sketch of a skin sensory neuron capable of responding (electrically) to an increase of pressure at that point. What causes that activity? Well, that neuron connects to the inside of the spinal medulla, where it makes contact with many interneurons. Among them, some make direct contact with a motoneuron capable, by its activity, of triggering the contraction of a muscle. This results in a movement. This movement results in a change of sensory activity by decreasing pressure on the sensory neuron; this reestablishes a certain reciprocal relation between the sensory and motor surfaces. Described from the outside, what happened is that the hand was withdrawn from a painful stimulus. Described from the nervous system, what happened is that a certain sensorimotor correlation was maintained within the nervous system through a neuronal network. Now, since many other neurons that originate in other parts of the nervous system (e.g., at the cortex) may influence the activity of the motoneurons, the behavior of leaving the hand under the excess pressure is also possible. But this would mean establishing a new internal balance, involving other neuronal groups more diverse than in the first case, where the hand was withdrawn.

Let us try to imagine, from particular situations like the previous example of painful pressure, an organism that functions normally. At each moment we shall find that the nervous system is operating according to many internal cycles of neuronal interactions (like that of the motoneurons and sensory fibers of the muscle) in never-ending change. Modulating this immense activity are those changes in the sensory surface due to perturbations independent of the organism (such as pressure on the skin). As observers, we are used to focusing our attention on what is more apparent to us, that is, external perturbations, and we readily believe that this is the determining factor. These external perturbations, however, as we just said, can only modulate the constant coming and going of internal balances of sensorimotor correlations.

This is an important notion that we can illustrate by what happens in the visual system. We commonly think that visual perception is a certain operation on the retinal image, whose representation will then be transformed inside the nervous system. This is the representationist approach to

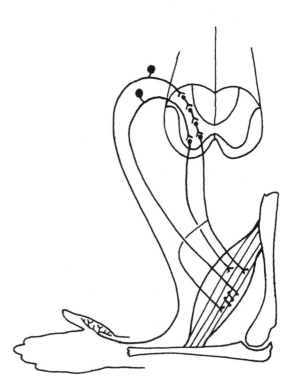

Fig. 47. Sensorimotor correlation in movement of the arm.

the phenomenon. This approach to the visual
phenomenon, however, is dispelled once we realize that for each neuron on the retina projected to
our visual cortex via the so-called lateral geniculate nucleus (LGN), there are hundreds of neurons from other zones of the nervous system,
including other cortical areas, that project to the
LGN. Thus, the LGN is not simply a relay station
for retinal projections to the cerebral cortex, since
many fibers from other parts of the brain converge
upon it and influence whatever comes out of it toward the visual cortex. This is shown in the box
entitled "Connections in the Visual Path." Note in
this diagram that one of the structures affecting
what happens in the LGN is the very same visual
cortex to which the cells of the LGN project. That
is, both structures are interrelated through reciprocal influences, and not in a simple sequential way.

Connections in the Visual Path

The diagram below shows the many connections in the geniculate nucleus of a
mammal. This nucleus is the most promi-
nent region of connections between the
retina and the central nervous system.
Each one of the names indicated in the diagram corresponds to some distinguishable
aggregate of neurons in different regions of
the central nervous system, including the
cerebral cortex. As is clear, the retina does
not affect the brain like a telephone line
that encounters a relay station at the LGN,
since more than 80 percent of the interconnections come together at the LGN at
the same time. Consequently, the retina
can modulate—but not specify—the state
of the neurons in the geniculate nucleus,
whose state will be given by all the connections it receives from many different parts
of the brain. A similar diagram (with other
names, of course) could be made for any
other center of the central nervous system.

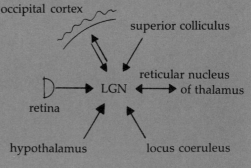

LGN = lateral geniculate nucleus

It is enough to contemplate this structure of the nervous system (even though we cannot know much in detail about the relations of activity that occur from moment to moment) to be convinced that the effect of projecting an image on the retina is not like an incoming telephone line. Rather, it is like a voice (perturbation) added to many voices during a hectic family discussion (relations of activity among all incoming convergent connections) in which the consensus of actions reached will not depend on what any particular member of the family says.

Operational Closure of the Nervous System

We said that behavior is a description an observer makes of the changes of state in a system with respect to an environment with which that system interacts. We said also that the nervous system does not invent behavior, but expands it dramatically. Let us clarify what we mean by this word "expands." It means that the nervous system emerges in the phylogenetic history of living beings like a network of special cells (neurons), which is embedded in the organism in such a way that it couples points in the sensory surfaces with points in the motor surfaces. Thus, with a network of neurons coming between this coupling, the field of possible sensorimotor correlations of the organism is increased and the realm of behavior is expanded.

It is now clear that the sensory surface includes not only those cells that we see externally as receptors capable of being perturbed by the environment, but also those cells capable of being perturbed by the organism itself, including the neuronal network. Thus, for instance, there are chemoreceptor cells in some arteries capable of being specifically modified by changes in the oxygen concentration of a vertebrate's blood. These cells, in turn, modify certain neurons that contribute by their change of activity to changes of state in the entire network leading to changes in the rhythm of activation of respiratory muscles, which thus affect the oxygen level in the blood. Thus the nervous system participates in the operation of a metacellular as a mechanism that maintains within certain limits the structural changes of the organism. This occurs through multiple circuits of neuronal activity structurally coupled to the medium. In this sense, the nervous system can be characterized as having *operational closure*. In other words, the nervous system's organization is a network of active components in which every change of relations of activity leads to further changes of relations of activity. Some of these relationships remain invariant through continuous perturbation both due to the nervous system's own dynamics and due to the interactions of the organism it integrates.

In other words, the nervous system functions as a closed network of changes in relations of activity between its components.

Thus, when we experience excessive pressure in any part of the body, as observers we can say: "Aha! The contracting of this muscle will cause me to lift my arm." But from the standpoint of the operation of the nervous system as such (like the case of our friend in the submarine), what occurs is only the constant maintenance of certain relations between sensory and motor elements that were temporarily perturbed by outside pressure.

Fig. 48. Relative size of the cephalic portion of the nervous system in various animals.

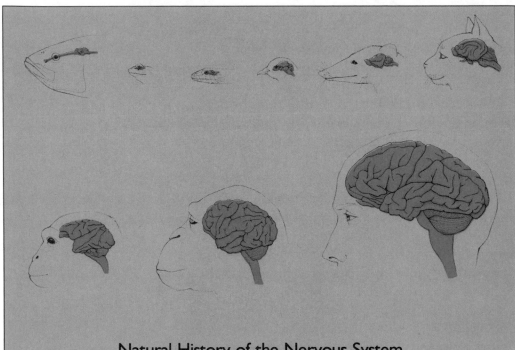

Natural History of the Nervous System

In coelenterates (the hydra) the nervous system is distributed evenly throughout the organism. Such is not the case with other animals, such as mammals. There are two basic trends in the transformation of the nervous system in the history of living beings: (1) uniting neurons in a compartment (nervous cord) and (2) concentrating a greater neuronal volume in the cephalic end (cephallization). Thus, in segmented animals, such as earthworms, there is a nervous system typically concentrated in cell groups in the form of ganglia segmentally distributed throughout the animal; however, these groups are interconnected with a slight cephalic concentration. In other animals, the cephalic concentration can be enormous, as clearly seen, for instance, in the octopus and, even more, in the human being.

The result of this is that the function of the nervous system diversifies tremendously with an increase in the variety of modes of neuronal interactions, which entails growth in the cephalic portion. We see this in all the lineages of vertebrates, mollusks, and insects (Fig. 43). In other words, this increase in cephalic mass carries with it enormous possibilities for structural plasticity of the organism. This is fundamental for the capacity to learn, and we shall return to this later.

The internal relationship maintained in this case is relatively simple: it is a balance between sensory activity and muscle tone. As to what determines the balance of muscle tone in relation to the rest of the nervous system's activity, it is hard to say in a few words. But, as a rule, all behavior is an outside view of the dance of internal relations of the organism. Finding out in each case the precise mechanisms of those neuronal coherences is the task that the researcher faces.

What we said shows that the operation of the nervous system is wholly consistent with its forming part of an autonomous unity in which every state of activity leads to another state of activity in the same unity, because its operation is circular, or in an operational closure. The nervous system, therefore, by its very architecture does not violate but enriches the operational closure that defines the autonomous nature of the living being. We begin to see clearly the ways in which every process of cognition is necessarily based on the organism as a unity and on the operational closure of its nervous system; hence it follows that all knowing is doing as sensory-effector correlations in the realms of structural coupling in which the nervous system exists.

Plasticity

Several times we mentioned the fact that the nervous system is a system in continuous structural change, that is, it has plasticity. Indeed, this is a basic dimension in its participating in the makeup of an organism. In effect, as a result of this structural plasticity, the nervous system, through its sensory and effector organs in the interactions of the organism that select its structural change, participates in the structural drift of the organism with conservation of its adaptation.

Now, the structural change of the nervous system does not normally occur as something radical in its broad lines of connectivity. These, on the whole, are invariant and generally they are the same in all individuals of one species. Between the fertilized zygote and the adult, in the process of development and cell differentiation, as the neurons multiply they begin to branch out and connect according to an architecture proper to the species. Exactly how this occurs by processes of exclusive local determination is one of the most interesting puzzles of modern biology.

Where do structural changes occur, therefore, if not in the broad lines of connectivity? The answer is that they occur, not in the connections that unite groups of neurons, but in the local characteristics of those connections. That is to say, changes occur in the final ramifications and in the synapses. There, molecular changes result in changes in the efficiency of the synaptic interactions that can modify drastically how the entire neuronal network functions.

For instance, let us picture the following experiment. We locate one of the big muscles that activate the leg of a mouse, isolating the nerve that descends from the spinal medulla and innervates the muscle. We then cut the nerve and allow the animal to recuperate. After some time, we reopen the animal and examine the muscle. We will find that it is atrophied and shortened. But we did not alter its aliment and blood supply. All we did was cut the electric and chemical traffic that normally exists between the muscle and the connecting nerve. If we allow the nerve to grow again and re-innervate the muscle, that muscle will recuperate and the atrophy will disappear. Other experiments show that something similar occurs between many (if not all) neuronal elements that make up the nervous system. The level of activity and the chemical traffic between two cells—in this case, a muscle fiber and a neuron—modulate the efficiency and mode of interaction between them during their continuous change. By cutting the nerve, we see this dynamic feature in a dramatic way.

The plasticity of the nervous system lies in the fact that the neurons are not connected as though they were cables with their respective plugs. The points of interaction between the cells are zones of delicate dynamic balance modulated by a great number of elements that trigger local structural changes, and that are produced as a result of the activity of those cells and of other cells whose products are released into the blood flow and wash the neurons. It is all part of the dynamics of interactions of the organism in its environment.

There is no known nervous system that does not show some degree of plasticity. But plasticity seems to be much more limited in certain organisms, for example, among insects, in part because they have fewer neurons and are smaller in size. Hence, the phenomenon of structural change manifests itself with vigor among vertebrates and particularly among mammals. Thus, there is no interaction and there is no coupling without consequence for the operation of the nervous system as a result of the structural changes triggered in it. We human beings in particular are modified by every experience, even though at times the changes are not wholly visible.

This we know mostly through observation of behavior. We do not have a clear picture today of structural changes in the nervous system of verte-

The Brain and the Computer

It is interesting to note that the operational closure of the nervous system tells us that it does not operate according to either of the two extremes: it is neither representational nor solipsistic.

It is not solipsistic, because as part of the nervous system's organism, it participates in the interactions of the nervous system in its environment. These interactions continuously trigger in it the structural changes that modulate its dynamics of states. In fact, this is the basis of why, as observers, we see animal behavior in general as being in line with its circumstances and why animals do not behave as though they were following their own leader independently of the environment. This is so despite the fact that, for the operation of the nervous system, there is no inside or outside, but only maintenance of correlations that continuously change (like the in-dicator instruments in the submarine we used as an example).

Nor is it representational, for in each interaction it is the nervous system's structural state that specifies what perturbations are possible and what changes trigger them. It would therefore be a mistake to define the nervous system as having inputs or outputs in the traditional sense. This would mean that such inputs or outputs are part of the definition of the system, as in the case of a computer or other machines that have been engineered. To do this is entirely reasonable when one has designed a machine whose central feature is the manner in which we interact with it. The nervous system (or the organism), however, has not been designed by anyone; it is the result of a phylogenic drift of unities centered on their own dynamics of states. What is necessary, therefore, is to recognize the nervous system as a unity defined by its internal relations in which interactions come into play only by modulating its structural dynamics, i.e., as a unity with operational closure. In other words, the nervous system does not "pick up information" from the environment, as we often hear. On the contrary, it brings forth a world by specifying what patterns of the environment are perturbations and what changes trigger them in the organism. The popular metaphor of calling the brain an "information-processing device" is not only ambiguous but patently wrong.

brates involved in this plasticity. Nor do we have a clear description of how this constant transformation of the mode of neuronal interaction (that occurs in the ontogenic structural drift of the organism) is coupled to ongoing behavior. Again, this is one of the most significant areas of research in neurobiology today.

But whatever may be the precise mechanisms
that come into play in this constant microscopic
transformation during the interactions of the organism, such changes can never be localized nor
seen as anything proper to each experience (e.g.,
one will never find the record of a dog's name inside
its head). This cannot be, first of all because the
structural changes triggered in the nervous system are necessarily distributed owing to changes
of relative activity in a neuronal network. Second,
because the behavior of responding to a name is
a description that an observer makes of certain
actions that result from certain sensorimotor
patterns which, by dint of their internal operation, involve (strictly speaking) the entire nervous
system.

The plastic splendor of the nervous system
does not lie in its production of "engrams" or representations of things in the world; rather, it lies in
its continuous transformation in line with transformations of the environment as a result of how
each interaction affects it. From the observer's
standpoint, this is seen as proportionate learning.
What is occurring, however, is that the neurons,
the organism they integrate, and the environment
in which they interact operate reciprocally as selectors of their corresponding structural changes
and are coupled with each other structurally: the
functioning organism, including its nervous system, selects the structural changes that permit it
to continue operating, or it disintegrates.

To an observer, the organism appears as moving
proportionately in a changing environment; and
he speaks of learning. To him, the structural
changes that occur in the nervous system seem to
correspond to the circumstances of the interactions of the organism. In terms of the nervous

system's operation, however, there is only an on-going structural drift that follows the course in which, at each instant, the structural coupling (adaptation) of the organism to its medium of interaction is conserved.

Innate Behavior and Learned Behavior

We have said many times—lest we forget—that all behavior is a relational phenomenon that we, as observers, witness between organisms and environment. An organism's range of possible behavior, however, is determined by its structure. This structure specifies its realms of interaction. For this reason, every time in the organisms of one species certain structures develop independently of the peculiarities of their histories of interaction, it is said that those structures are genetically determined and that the behavior they make possible (if any) is *instinctive*. When an infant shortly after being born suckles its mother's breast, it does so independently of whether it was born by natural delivery or caesarian section, or whether it was born in a highly efficient urban hospital or on a remote island.

But if the structures that make possible a certain behavior in members of one species develop only if there is a particular history of interactions, it is said that the structures are ontogenic and the behavior is *learned*. The wolf girl mentioned in the last chapter did not have the social interactions that every child has, and her ability to run on two feet, for instance, never developed. Even in something as elemental as running, we depend on a human context that surrounds us like the air we breathe.

Note well that innate behavior and learned behavior are, as behaviors, indistinguishable in their nature and in their embodiment. The distinction lies in the history of the structures that make them possible. Therefore, our classifying them as one or the other depends on whether or not we have access to the pertinent structural history. We cannot make that distinction by observing the operation of the nervous system in the present.

It is important to realize that we tend to consider learning and memory as phenomena of changing conduct related to "taking in" or receiving something from the environment. This presupposes that the nervous system functions with representations. We have already seen that this supposition obscures and complicates tremendously our understanding of the cognitive processes. Everything we have said points to learning as an expression of structural coupling, which always maintains compatibility between the operation of the organism and its environment. When we as observers look at a sequence of perturbations, for which the nervous system compensates in one of many possible ways, it seems to us that it internalizes something of the environment. But, as we know, to make this description would undermine our logical accounting: as though something useful to us for communication between observers were an operational element of the nervous system. To describe learning as an internalization of the environment confuses things by suggesting that in the structural dynamics of the nervous system there are phenomena that exist only in the descriptive realms of some organisms, like ourselves, capable of language.

Knowledge and Nervous System

In the previous chapter we talked about realms of behavior. In this chapter we have talked about the basic organization of the nervous system. Thus, we have come ever closer to those everyday phenomena that we call acts of knowledge. We are now ready to refine our understanding about what is meant when we say that an act is cognitive.

If we reflect a moment on what criterion we are using to say whether someone *has* knowledge, we will see that what we are seeking is an effective action in the realm where an answer is expected. That is, we are expecting an effective behavior in a context that we specify with our question. Thus, two observations made about the same subject, under the same conditions, but with different questions, can render different cognitive values about the behavior of the subject.

A story from real life illustrates this clearly. A university student was told during an examination: "Calculate the height of the university tower by using this altimeter." The student took the altimeter and a long string, went to the top of the tower, tied the altimeter to the string, and dropped it very carefully to the foot of the tower. He then measured the length of the cord that extended to the bottom. It measured 30 meters and 40 centimeters. The professor, however, considered his answer wrong. But the student was given another chance. Again the professor told him: "Calculate the height of the university tower with this altimeter." The young student took the altimeter, went to the garden near the tower with a goniometer. Standing at a certain distance from the tower, he used the length of the altimeter to triangulate the tower. He calculated 30 meters and 15 centimeters. The professor again said he was

Knowledge

We admit knowledge whenever we observe an effective (or adequate) behavior in a given context, i.e., in a realm or domain which we define by a question (explicit or implicit).

wrong. The student was given another chance. Again, the same problem. The student used six different procedures to calculate the tower's height with the altimeter, without ever using it as an altimeter. Evidently, from a certain standpoint, the pupil revealed much more knowledge than he was asked for. From the standpoint of the professor's question, his knowledge was inadequate.

Note well, therefore, that the evaluation of whether or not there is knowledge is made always in a relational context. In that context, the structural changes which perturbations trigger in an organism appear to the observer as an effect upon the environment. It is in reference to the effect the observer expects that he assesses the structural changes triggered in the organism. From that standpoint, every interaction of an organism, every behavior observed, *can* be assessed by an observer as a cognitive act. In the same way, the fact of living—of conserving structural coupling uninterruptedly as a living being—is to *know* in the realm of existence. In a nutshell: to live is to know (living is effective action in existence as a living being).

In principle, this is sufficient to explain the nervous system's participation in all cognitive dimensions. But if we wish to understand the nervous system's participation in all the particular forms of human knowledge, of course we would have to describe all the specific and concrete processes involved in generating each human behavior in its different realms of structural coupling. For that, it would be necessary to look closely at the operation of the nervous system in human beings, in full detail; but that is beyond the scope of this book.

To sum up: the nervous system participates in cognitive phenomena in two complementary ways. These have to do with its particular mode of operation as a neuronal network with operational closing as part of a metacellular system.

The first, and most obvious, is through expanding the realm of possible states of the organism that arises from the great diversity of sensorimotor patterns which the nervous system allows for and which is the key to its participation in the operation of the organism.

The second is through opening new dimensions of structural coupling for the organism, by making possible in the organism the association of many different internal states with the different interactions in which the organism is involved.

The presence or absence of a nervous system determines any discontinuity between organisms that have a cognition relatively restricted and those that are open-ended, as in human beings. To point up its key importance, to the symbol that designates an autopoietic (cellular or multicellular) unity:

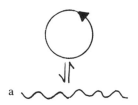

we must now add the presence of a nervous system, which functions also with operational closure but as an integral part of the organism. We diagram it succinctly as follows:

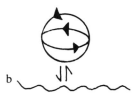

In an organism with a nervous system rich and vast as that of human beings, its realms of interaction open the way to *new phenomena* by allowing new dimensions of structural coupling. In human beings, this makes for language and self-consciousness. This is the terrain we shall explore in the next chapters.

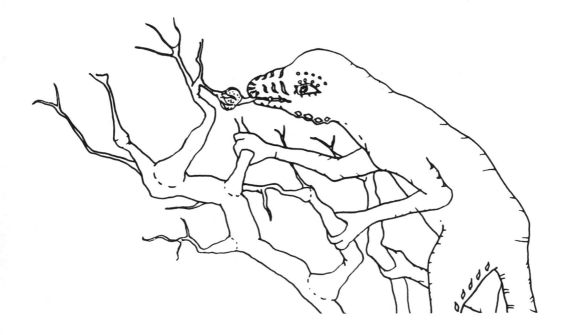

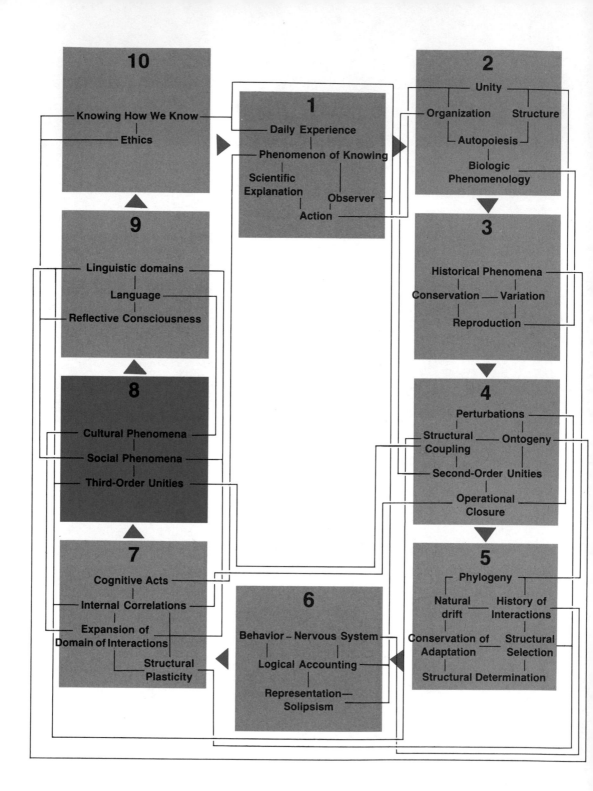

10

Knowing How We Know
Ethics

1

Daily Experience
Phenomenon of Knowing
Scientific
Explanation
Observer
Action

2

Unity
Organization Structure
Autopoiesis
Biologic
Phenomenology

3

Historical Phenomena
Conservation — Variation
Reproduction

9

Linguistic domains
Language
Reflective Consciousness

8

Cultural Phenomena
Social Phenomena
Third-Order Unities

4

Perturbations
Structural Ontogeny
Coupling
Second-Order Unities
Operational
Closure

7

Cognitive Acts
Internal Correlations
Expansion of
Domain of Interactions
Structural
Plasticity

6

Behavior – Nervous System
Logical Accounting
Representation—
Solipsism

5

Phylogeny
Natural History of
drift Interactions
Conservation of Structural
Adaptation Selection
Structural Determination

8　Social Phenomena

Fig. 49. Drawing by Juste de
Juste.

Let us consider a situation parallel to that in Chapter 4 as regards the origin of metacellulars. That is, instead of looking at an organism only with its nervous system,

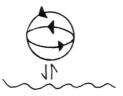

let us look at what happens when this organism enters into structural coupling with other organisms.

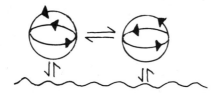

As in the case of cellular interactions in metacellulars, it is evident that from the standpoint of the internal dynamics of one organism, the other represents a source of perturbations indistinguishable from those that come from a "nonbiotic" environment. It is *possible*, however, for these interactions between organisms to acquire in the course of their ontogeny a *recurrent* nature. This will necessarily result in their consequent structural drifts: co-ontogenies with mutual involvement through their reciprocal structural coupling, each one conserving its adaptation and organization. When this happens, the co-drifting organisms give rise to a *new phenomenological domain*, which may become particularly complex when there is a nervous system. The phenomena arising from these *third-order structural couplings* will be the subject of this chapter and the next.

Third-Order Couplings

At this point in our discussion, it should not be surprising that third-order couplings can occur, because these are basically the same mechanisms we discussed in relation to the makeup of second-order autopoietic unities. In fact, once organisms with a nervous system arise, if the organisms take part in recurrent interactions, these couplings will occur—with definite complexity and stability, but as a natural result of the congruence of their respective ontogenic drifts. How can we better understand these third-order couplings?

In the first place, we must realize that such couplings are absolutely necessary for the continuity of a lineage in organisms with sexual reproduction, for gametes have to meet and merge. In addition, in many animals that require mating for the procreation of new individuals, the young need some care by their parents. Hence, some degree of behavioral coupling is common in the generating and rearing of the young.

Now, since third-order couplings are a relatively universal phenomenon, they occur in different animal groups under a variety of forms. These forms differ both in how they occur and in the additional phenomena they give rise to. As human beings brought up in a patriarchal culture, we tend to think that it is natural for the female to care for her young and for the male to look after their protection and sustenance. Supposedly, this image is based in part on the fact that we are mammals with more or less long periods of breastfeeding during which rearing is necessarily associated with the mother. There is no mammal species in which nursing is the male's responsibility.

This clear-cut division of roles, however, is far from universal. Thus, among birds we find a very great variety of roles. For instance, both the male and female can produce a kind of milky product in their craw which they regurgitate for the young. In other cases, it is the male who cares for the eggs and the young, for example, among South American ostriches, where the male mates with a harem of females (polygyny), each of which lays an egg in a hole. Once it is filled, the male diligently takes charge.

This domestic inclination of the male is found in a more mixed form in another South American bird, the jacaña. In this case, the female marks out a more or less vast territory. She prepares several nests and allows entrance to the same number of males (polyandry). After fertilization, she lays an egg in each one of the nests and builds a nest for herself, where she lays another egg. In this way, both females and males have the pleasure of rearing the chicks (Fig. 50).

Fig. 50. Jacaña.

Among penguins, there is an even more striking variation. In this case, getting food for the young is apparently more difficult and requires the participation of both parents. What care is given to the little penguins? It is interesting to note: as parents leave in search of food, some of the adults in the group stay close by and take care of the whole group; they form a veritable kindergarten.

Among fish, the stickleback is an extreme case. It is the male that builds a nest, lures the female to lay her eggs in it, then drives her out (Fig. 51). Once alone, the male carefully circulates water to

Fig. 51. Aspects of courting
behavior in the stickleback.

bathe the eggs by swinging his tail until they hatch. After that, he looks after the little fish until they are on their own. That is to say, in this case it is the male who takes charge of rearing. His relationship with the female lasts only as long as courtship and egg-laying.

There are other examples in which it is the female who has greater responsibility in rearing. We could continue to give many examples of the necessary coupling of procreation and rearing. Evidently there are no fixed roles. Nor are there any in human societies, where there are many cases of polyandry and polygyny and where sharing of the tasks of rearing the young varies from one extreme to the other. In fact, much of the diversity of the third-order coupling in which we participate rests on the immense diversity of behavioral couplings afforded by the nervous system. We must keep this well in mind, to understand human social dynamics as a biologic phenomenon.

Social Insects

Sexual and rearing behavioral couplings are essentially transitory. There are many other kinds of behavioral coupling. These can go much further toward specifying, among individuals of one group, behavioral coordinations that can last a lifetime.

The classic and more notable example of a third-order coupling that involves the entire ontogeny of participating organisms is that of social insects. These animals comprise many species among varied orders of insects. In many of them, very similar mechanisms have arisen in parallel ways. Well-known examples of social insects are ants, termites, wasps, and bees.

For instance, Figure 52 shows different individuals found among myrmicine ants, one of the well-studied groups. We see there is a great variety of forms among the participating individuals. Their morphologies have a marked differentiation as to their activities in the colony. Thus, most of the individuals in Fig. 52 are barren females; their tasks are to store food, defend the colony, take care of the eggs, and maintain the anthill. The males are secluded inside, where usually there is only one fertile female, the queen (marked *g* in Fig. 52). Remarkable among the barren females are those with enormous mandibles, capable of

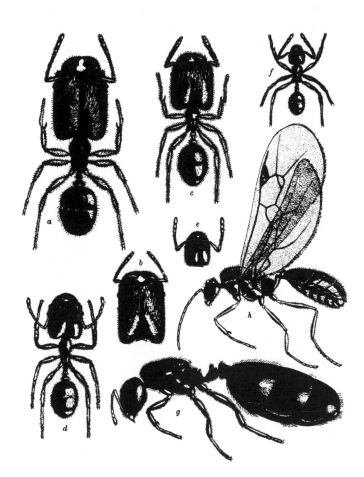

Fig. 52. Different morphologies in the castes of myrmicine ants (*Pheidole kingi instabilis*). Individuals of the worker caste are shown in (a) through (f). The queen is shown in (g) and the male in (h).

exerting great pressure. They are much bigger than the worker females (*e* and *f*). Most of the ants in an anthill like this have no participation at all in reproduction. This is reserved for the queen and the males; however, all individuals in the anthill are coupled in their structural dynamics and do not survive (or survive for only a short time) if permanently isolated.

The *mechanism* of structural coupling among most social insects takes place through the interchange of substances. Therefore, it is a chemical coupling. In fact, there is a continuous flow of secretions between the members of an ant colony through sharing of stomach contents each time they meet. We can observe this act by following a line of ants in a garden. From this continuous chemical flow, called *trophallaxis* (Fig. 53), results the distribution, throughout the population, of an amount of substances (among them, hormones) responsible for the differentiation and specification of roles. Thus, the queen is a queen as long as she is fed in a certain way and certain substances that she produces are distributed among the colony members. Remove the queen from her location, and immediately the hormonal imbalance that her absence causes will result in a change in the feeding of the larvae which develop into queens. Indeed, all the ontogenies of the different members of an ant colony are bound together in a co-ontogenic structural drift as they arise in a network of continuously changing trophallactic interactions. In an ant colony, the ontogeny of each individual is contingent on the ontogenies of the others.

Actually, the detailed processes and mechanisms that determine castes, modes of cooperation between different species, territorial organi-

Fig. 53. Mechanism of coupling between social insects:
trophallaxis.

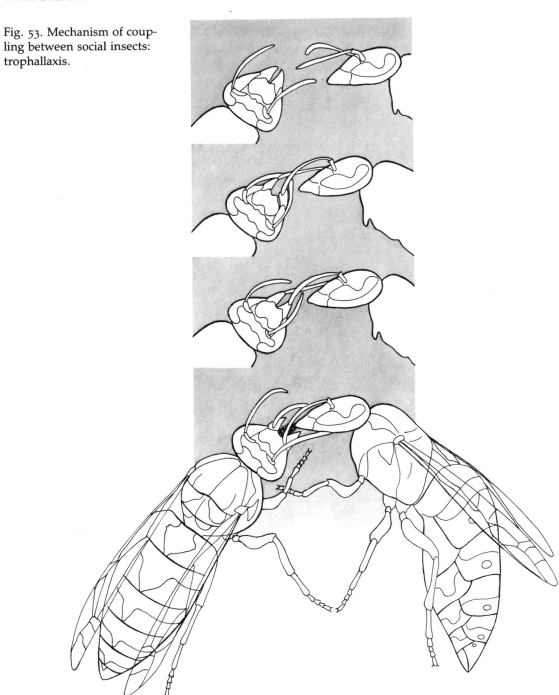

zation, and many other aspects in the life of social insects have motivated many studies and are an ever-renewed source of circumstances that reveal the most unexpected forms of structural coupling among these organisms. In all these circumstances, however, we note a degree of rigidity and inflexibility. This should not be too surprising, as insects (like many other invertebrates) are essentially organized on the basis of an outer armor of chitin. Imbedded in that armor are the muscles that move it. This architecture entails a limitation in the maximum size that insects can reach, hence in the size of the nervous system they possess. Accordingly, insects are not distinguished individually by their behavioral variety and capacity to learn. Vertebrates, however, with their inner skeleton on which their muscles depend, are capable of prolonged growth; they are not so restricted in size. This permits larger organisms (more cells) with larger nervous systems, which makes possible a greater diversity of states, as also greater behavioral diversity.

Social Vertebrates

Let us imagine a herd of ungulates such as the antelopes, which live in the mountains. If we have ever had occasion to approach them, we noticed that as soon as we got within a hundred yards, the whole herd fled. Usually they flee until they reach a somewhat higher peak. From there, they look out and observe once again. To go from one peak to another, however, they have to pass through a valley that impedes their view of the onlooker. Here we see a clear case of social coupling: the herd moves in a formation led by the dominant male, followed by the females and the young. Other males bring up the rear, and one of them stays behind on the closest peak, to keep an eye on the stranger while the others descend. As soon as they have reached the new height, he joins them (Fig. 54).

As in the case of social insects, life in third-order couplings, or social life for short, permits individual vertebrates (a mammal in the above example) to participate in relations and activities that arise only as coordinations of behaviors between otherwise independent organisms. Such coordination can take place through any form of interaction: chemical, visual, auditory, and so on.

The structural differences involved in the different roles enacted by the members of groups in mammals frequently seem to us to be less striking than those exhibited by ants or termites because they involve more fleeting changes of shape and attitude, rather than permanent transformations of body appearance. That was the case with the alert young male antelope guarding the herd. It is

Fig. 54. Flight as a social phenomenon among deer.

also the case with wolves, which coordinate their behavior by adopting different postures (showing their teeth, drooping their ears, wagging their tails). The wolf pack, thus constituted, is capable of following, harassing, and killing a large moose (Fig. 55), a feat that could not be achieved by a single individual. Wolves are a good example of the flexibility that mammals exhibit to attain the coordination of their behavior.

We see among these vertebrates different modes of interaction fundamentally visual and auditory. This interaction enables them to generate a new realm of phenomena that isolated individuals cannot generate. In this respect, they resemble social insects. But they are different owing to the greater flexibility that their nervous system and visual-auditory coupling gives them.

Fig. 55. Hunting as a social phenomenon among wolves.

Fig. 56. A group of baboons on the move.

Among primates, comparable situations arise. For instance, the baboons that live in the savannas of Africa and that have been carefully studied as to their natural group behavior (very different from their behavior in captivity) manifest an ongoing and multiple interaction that is gestural, postural (visual), and tactile.[9] It is a dynamic system of hierarchical relations. This system of hierarchical relations defines the cohesion of the group, which is apparent when they migrate from one place to another or confront a predator such as a lion. When the group migrates, the dominant males and females and the young go to the center. Other males, adults and youngsters, and females strategically position themselves in the front and rear (Fig. 56). For many hours of the day, the baboons play and groom each other in continuous interaction. Within these groups, we note the ex-

9. I. DeVore and K. R. Hall in *Primate Behavior* (New York: Holt, Reinhardt & Winston, 1965), pp. 20–53.

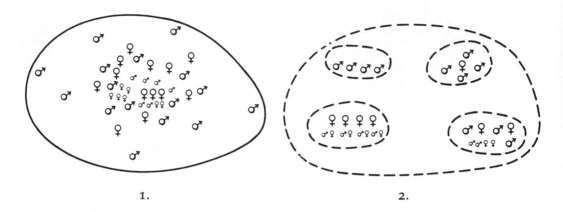

pression of what we could call individual temperaments: some baboons are irritable, others seductive, still others are explorers, and so on. All this behavioral diversity gives to each group of baboons its own stamp; each individual is continually adjusting its position in the network of interactions that forms the group according to its own dynamics, owing to its history of structural coupling in the group. Despite the differences, there is a style of organization in the group of baboons, a style that is generalized from group to group; therefore, it reflects the phylogenic lineage shared by them all.

Different groups of primates show varied modes and styles of interaction. The sacred baboons of North Africa are usually very aggressive and their hierarchies very rigid. Chimpanzees, however, live a more fluid network in a less assertive hierarchy. This allows for extended family groups and a great internal individual mobility (Fig. 57). Thus, each group of primates has its own features.

Fig. 57. Comparative sketch of distribution of baboon and chimpanzee individuals.

1. Structure that corresponds to baboons that inhabit the savanna

2. Structure that corresponds to chimpanzees in the jungle

————Frontier of a closed group
----------Frontier of an open group

Social Phenomena and Communication

We call social phenomena those phenomena that arise in the spontaneous constitution of third-order couplings, and social systems the third-order unities that are thus constituted. The form embodied by unities of this class varies considerably from insects to ungulates to primates. What is common to them all is that whenever they arise—if only to last for a short time—they generate a particular internal phenomenology, namely, one in which *the individual ontogenies of all the participating organisms occur fundamentally as part of the network of co-ontogenies that they bring about in constituting third-order unities.*

Since the constitution of a social system entails the actual co-ontogeny of its components, it entails their reciprocal structural coupling; and any particular organism is a member of a social unity only as long as it forms part of that reciprocal structural coupling. Therefore, as observers we can describe a behavior of reciprocal coordination between them. We call *communication* the coordinated behaviors mutually triggered among the members of a social unity. In this way, we understand as communication a particular type of behavior, with or without the presence of the nervous system, in the operation of the organisms in social systems. And, as with all behaviors, if we can distinguish the instinctive or learned nature of social behavior, we can distinguish also between phylogenic and ontogenic forms of communication.

The particular feature of communication, therefore, is not that it results from a mechanism distinct from other behaviors, but that it takes place in a domain of social behaviors. This applies equally to us as describers of our social behavior, whose complexity does not signify that our nervous system operates in a distinctive way.

A beautiful case of nonhuman communication is the singing of certain birds, such as the parrot and its close relatives. These animals ordinarily live in a dense forest with little or no visual contact. Under these conditions, mating couples form and coordinate through producing a common song. For instance, Figure 58 shows a spectrogram of two African birds. (A spectrogram is a way of taking sound and putting it on paper in two dimensions, as a continuous musical notation.) From the spectrogram, it seems that each bird is singing a full melody. It is not so, however, and it is possible to show that this melody is actually a duet: each member of a couple builds a phrase which the other continues. This melody is peculiar to each couple and is defined during the history of their mating. In this case (unlike what happens with many other birds), the vocal coordination of behavior in the singing couple is an ontogenic phenomenon.

What we wish to stress here is that the particular melody of each couple in this species of bird is

The Cultural Phenomena

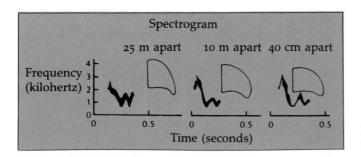

Fig. 58. Vocal duet between two African birds.

Social Phenomena

We call *social phenomena* those phenomena associated with the participation of organisms in constituting third-order unities.

Communication

As observers we designate as *communicative* those behaviors which occur in social coupling, and as *communication* that behavioral coordination which we observe as a result of it.

unique to its history of coupling. Moreover, the offspring of this coupling, in their own mating behavior, produce melodies different from those of their parents. The particular melody of each couple is limited to the life of the participating individuals.

This situation is quite different from that other behavior (also clearly ontogenic) which we can illustrate by an anecdote from England. Not many years ago, in metropolitan London, new milk bottles capped with thin aluminum covers instead of stiff cardboard were introduced. This new cover was thin enough to be pierced by a bird's beak. And so, a short time after this change, some birds—blue titmice—learned how to puncture the covers and feed on the top layer of cream. What is interesting is that behavior spread from this focal point to all the British Isles. In a short while, all blue

The Metaphor of the Tube for Communication

Our discussion has led us to conclude that, biologically, there is no "transmitted information" in communication. Communication takes place each time there is behavioral coordination in a realm of structural coupling.

This conclusion is surprising only if we insist on not questioning the latest metaphor for communication which has become popular with the so-called communication media. According to this metaphor of the tube, communication is something generated at a certain point. It is carried by a conduit (or tube) and is delivered to the receiver at the other end. Hence, there is a *something* that is communicated, and what

is communicated is an integral part of that which travels in the tube. Thus, we usually speak of the "information" contained in a picture, an object, or, more evidently, the printed word.

According to our analysis, this metaphor is basically false. It presupposes a unity that is not determined structurally, where interactions are instructive, as though what happens to a system in an interaction is determined by the perturbing agent and not by its structural dynamics. It is evident, however, even in daily life, that such is not the case with communication: each person says what he says or hears what he hears according to his own structural determination; saying does not ensure listening. From the perspective of an observer, there is always ambiguity in a communicative interaction. The phenomenon of communication depends on not what is transmitted, but on what happens to the person who receives it. And this is a very different matter from "transmitting information."

titmice had learned the trick of getting a good breakfast.

Vertebrates have an essential and unique capacity: imitation. Exactly what imitation is in terms of nervous physiology is not easy to say. But in terms of behavior it is obvious. Because of this phenomenon called imitation, what began as a behavior centered on some blue titmice expanded rapidly. Imitation therefore permits a certain mode of interaction to go beyond the ontogeny of one individual; it remains more or less invariant through successive generations. If the chicks of the titmice could not imitate, the habit of eating cream from the bottles would have to be invented anew in each generation.

Altruism and Selfishness

A study of the ontogenic couplings between organisms and an assessment of their great universality and variety point to a peculiar social phenomenon. We can say that when an antelope stays behind and takes a greater risk than the others, it is the group which benefits and not necessarily that antelope. We can also say that when a worker ant does not reproduce but goes about getting food for all the offspring on the anthill, once again it is the group which benefits and not that ant directly.

It is as though there were a balance between individual maintenance and subsistence and the maintenance and subsistence of the group as a greater unity that encompasses the individual. In fact, there is a balance between individual and group in natural drift as long as the organisms through their structural coupling into higher-order unities (which have their own realm of existence) include the maintenance of these unities in the dynamics of their own maintenance.

Ethologists have termed "altruistic" those actions that can be described as beneficial to the group. They have chosen a name that evokes a form of human behavior charged with ethical connotations. This may be so because biologists have long lived with a view of nature as "red in the tooth and in the claw," as a contemporary of Darwin said. We often hear that what Darwin proposed has to do with the law of the jungle because each one looks out for his own interests, selfishly, at the expense of others in unmitigated competition.

This view of animal life as selfish is doubly wrong. It is wrong, first, because natural history tells us, wherever we look, that instances of behavior which can be described as altruistic are almost universal. Second, it is wrong because the mechanisms we put forward to understand animal drift do not presuppose the individualistic view that the benefit of one individual requires the detriment of another.

Indeed, throughout this book we have seen that the existence of living organisms in natural drift (both ontogenic and phylogenic) is not geared to competition but to conservation of adaptation, in an individual encounter with the environment that results in survival of the fittest. Now, we as observers can change our frame of reference in our observation. We can consider also the group unity which individuals are a component of. In doing so, we see that the group necessarily conserves adaptation and organization in its realm of existence. In that group as a unity, individual components are irrelevant, for they can all be replaced by others that fulfill the same relations. For components as living beings, however, their individuality is their very condition for existence. It is important not to confuse these two phenomenal levels, to fully understand social phenomena. The behavior of the antelope that stays behind has to do with conservation of the group; it expresses characteristics proper of antelopes in their group coupling as long as the group exists as a unity. At the same time, this altruistic behavior in the individual antelope as regards group unity results from its structural coupling in an environment that includes the group; it is an expression of conservation of its adaptation as an individual. There is no contradiction, therefore, in the antelope's behavior insofar as it expresses individuality as a member of the group: it is "altruistically" selfish and "selfishly" altruistic, because its expression includes its structural coupling in the group it belongs to.

All these remarks are valid also in the human realm; however, they must be modified according to the features of the language as a mode of human social coupling. We shall see this later on.

Organisms and Societies

Organisms and societies belong to one class of metasystems; these consist of aggregates of autonomous unities that can be cellular or metacellular. An observer can distinguish the different metasystems of this class by the different degrees of autonomy he sees possible in their components. Thus, if he should put them in a series according to the degree of dependency of their components (in their embodiment as autonomous unities) on their participation in the metasystem they form, organisms and human social systems would be at the opposite ends of the series. Organisms would be metasystems of components with minimum autonomy, i.e., components with very little or no dimension of independent existence. Human societies, however, would be metasystems of components with maximum autonomy, i.e., components with many dimensions of independent existence. Societies made up of other metacellulars, such as insect societies, would be located at different intermediate points. The differences between these metasystems, however, are operational. Given some transformations in the respective internal and relational dynamics, they can move in one direction or other within the series. Let us look now at the differences between organisms and human social systems.

As metacellular systems, organisms have operational closure in the reciprocal structural coupling of their component cells. The central feature in the organization of an organism lies in its manner of being a unity in an environment wherein it must operate with stable properties that permit it to conserve its adaptation, whatever the properties of its components may be. This has a basic evolutionary consequence, viz., the conservation of adaptation of organisms in a particular lineage selects, recurrently, stabilization of the properties of their component cells. The genetic and ontogenetic stability of the cell processes that constitute the organisms of each species and the existence of organic processes that can eliminate abnormal cells reveal that this is so.

In human social systems, the case is different. As human communities these systems have operational closure, too, in the structural coupling of their components. But human social systems exist also as unities for their components in the realm of language. Therefore, the identity of human social systems depends on the conservation of adaptation of human beings not only as organisms (in a general sense) but also as components of their linguistic domains. Now, the evolutionary history of human beings is associated with their linguistic behavior. It is a history wherein that ontogenic behavioral plasticity is chosen which makes linguistic domains possible and wherein the conservation of adaptation of human beings as organisms requires their operation in those domains and the conservation of that plasticity. Just as the existence of an organism requires the operational stability of its components, the existence of a human social system requires the operational (behavioral) plasticity of those components. Just as organisms require nonlinguistic structural coupling between their components, human social systems require components structurally coupled in linguistic domains, where they (the components) can operate with language and be observers. Consequently, essential to the operation of an

organism is the organism itself; from it results limitation of the properties of its components. On the other hand, central to the operation of a human social system is the linguistic domain that its components generate and the extension of their properties—a condition necessary for the embodiment of language, which is their realm or domain of existence. The organism restricts the individual creativity of its component unities, as these unities exist for that organism. The human social system amplifies the individual creativity of its components, as that system exists for these components.

Coherence and harmony in relations and interactions between the components of each particular organism, in its development as an individual, are due to genetic and ontogenetic factors that restrict the structural plasticity of its components. Coherence and harmony in relations and interactions between the members of a human social system are due to the coherence and harmony of their growth in it, in an ongoing social learning which their own social (linguistic) operation defines and which is possible thanks to the genetic and ontogenetic processes that permit structural plasticity of the members.

Organisms and human social systems, therefore, are opposite cases in the series of metasystems formed by the aggregation of cellular systems of any order. Among them we have (besides different types of social systems made up of other animals) those human communities which, because they embody enforced mechanisms of stabilization in all the behavioral dimensions of their members, constitute impaired human social systems: they have lost their vigor and have depersonalized their components; they have become more like an organism, as in the case of Sparta. Organisms and human social systems cannot be compared without distorting or negating the features proper to their respective components.

Any analysis of human social phenomena that does not include these considerations will be defective, for it negates the biologic roots of those phenomena.

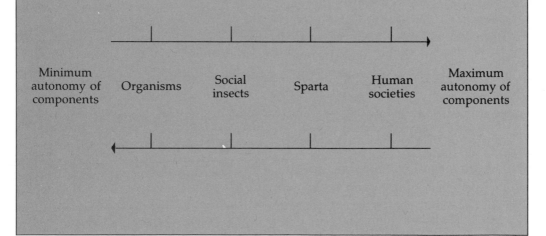

Fig. 59. A Japanese macaque washing its potatoes.

One of the most famous cases of social transgenerational permanency of learned behavior took place during some zoological studies that were done on a colony of wild macaques inhabiting a subtropical Japanese island (Fig. 59).[10] As part of the process of studying the macaque, the investigators left potatoes and corn on the beach. In this way, the monkeys, who normally inhabit the jungle next to the sea, went to the beach, where they were more visible. After a time, the macaques became more and more familiar with the sand, rocks, and sea. One of the observations made during these transformations was that a bright female, called Imo, one day discovered that she could wash potatoes in the water, thus cleaning off the sand, which made them unpleasant to eat. In a matter of days, the other macaques, es-

10. S. Kawamura, *Journal of Primatology* 2(1959):43.

Cultural Behavior

By *cultural behavior* we mean the transgenerational stability of behavioral patterns ontogenically acquired in the communicative dynamics of a social environment.

pecially the young ones, imitated Imo and were washing their potatoes. Furthermore, in the space of a few months, this new behavior extended to all the adjacent colonies.

Imo proved to be a very clever macaque. Some months later, after she had invented the washing of potatoes, she invented another behavior. She took wheat mixed with sand (hence hard to eat) and threw it into the water. She gathered up the floating wheat after the sand had submerged. This second invention, too, was gradually adopted by other colonies on the island. The older monkeys were always the slowest to acquire this new form of behavior.

Those behavioral patterns which have been acquired ontogenically in the communicative dynamics of a social environment and which have been stable through generations, we shall call *cultural* behaviors. This name should not be surprising, for it refers to the whole body of ontogenically acquired communicative interactions that give a certain continuity to the history of a group, beyond the particular history of the participating individuals. Imitation and ongoing intragroup behavioral selection play a key role here, resulting in the coupling of the young and adults. This leads to a certain ontogeny which we call culture in the human domain. Cultural behavior, therefore, is not a form essentially different from other learned behaviors. It is peculiar in that it arises as a consequence of social living over many generations while its members are continuously replaced.

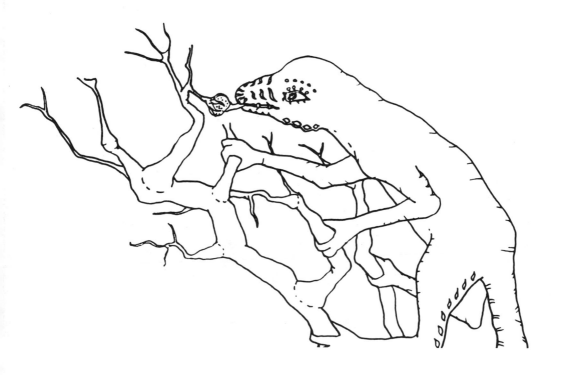

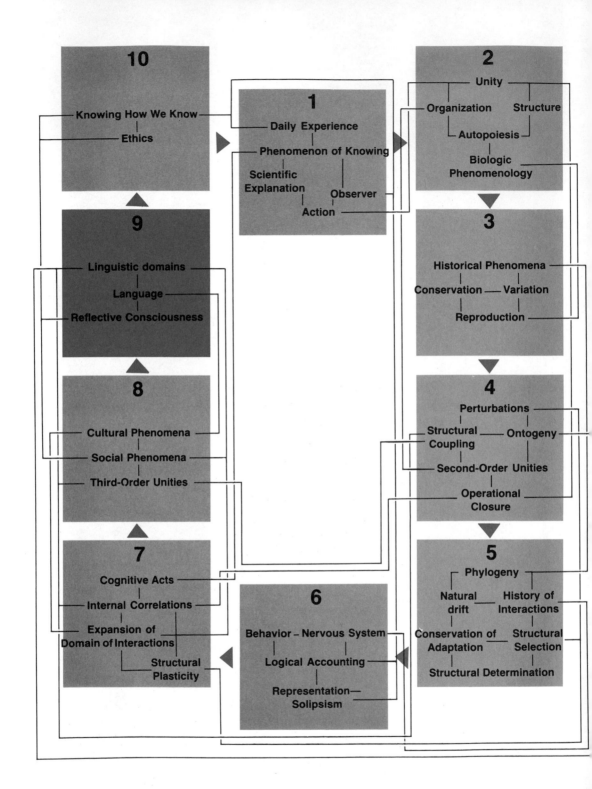

10
Knowing How We Know
Ethics

1
Daily Experience
Phenomenon of Knowing
Scientific
Explanation
Observer
Action

2
Unity
Organization — Structure
Autopoiesis
Biologic
Phenomenology

3
Historical Phenomena
Conservation — Variation
Reproduction

9
Linguistic domains
Language
Reflective Consciousness

8
Cultural Phenomena
Social Phenomena
Third-Order Unities

4
Perturbations
Structural — Ontogeny
Coupling
Second-Order Unities
Operational
Closure

7
Cognitive Acts
Internal Correlations
Expansion of
Domain of Interactions
Structural
Plasticity

6
Behavior – Nervous System
Logical Accounting
Representation—
Solipsism

5
Phylogeny
Natural — History of
drift — Interactions
Conservation of — Structural
Adaptation — Selection
Structural Determination

Linguistic Domains and Human Consciousness

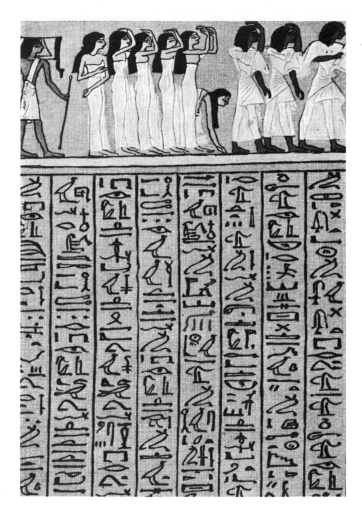

Fig. 60. Egyptian hieroglyphs.

A friend of ours was awakened each morning at dawn by his cat walking on the piano. When our friend got up, he found the animal standing next to the door leading out to the garden, which it would jauntily head for. If the man did not get up, the cat would walk again on the piano and make unharmonious sounds.

It seems quite natural to describe this behavior of the cat as "signaling" to our friend its desire to go out to the garden. This is tantamount to a *semantic* description of the behaviors of our friend and his cat. We know, however, that the interactions between them occurred only as a mutual triggering of changes of state as determined by their respective structures. Once again we must keep our logical accounting very clear and walk on the razor's edge, keeping the operation of an organism distinct from the description of its behavior.

Doubtless there are many cases, like that of our friend, in which we can apply a semantic description to a social phenomenon. We often do this by taking literary or metaphoric license. This makes the situation comparable to a human linguistic interaction, as in fairy tales. All this calls for closer examination on our part.

Semantic Descriptions

We saw in the last chapter that when two or more organisms interact recurrently, they generate a social coupling. In that coupling they are reciprocally involved in attaining their respective poieses. Behaviors that take place in these domains of social coupling, as we said, are communicative and they can be inborn or acquired. Both instinctive and learned behavior can appear to an observer as coordinations of action, and both can be described by an observer in semantic terms as if what determines the course of the interaction were the meaning and not the dynamics of structural coupling of the interacting organisms. These two kinds of communicative behavior differ, however, in the structures that make them possible. Innate behaviors depend on structures that arise in the development of the organism independently of its particular ontogeny. Acquired communicative behaviors depend on the particular ontogeny of the organism and are contingent on its peculiar history of social interactions. In this latter case, the observer can easily make a semantic description, claiming that the meaning of the different communicative behaviors arises in the ontogeny of the participant organisms, contingent on their particular history of coexistence. We call such learned communicative behavior a *linguistic domain*, because such behaviors constitute the basis for language, but they are not yet identical with it.

The reader does not need examples of linguistic domains. In the last chapter we saw several of them. We did not present them as such, because our topic was social phenomena in general. For instance, singing a duet is an elegant example of linguistic interaction. It is a good exercise for the reader to go back and look over the last chapter, to discover which of the communicative behaviors described can be treated as linguistic and to see how easy it is to describe them in semantic terms.

Let us note that the choice of this name—like the name "cognitive act," as we saw before—was not arbitrary. It is equivalent to saying that human linguistic behaviors are in fact behaviors in a domain of reciprocal ontogenic structural coupling which we human beings establish and maintain as a result of our collective co-ontogenies. In other words, when we describe words as designators of objects or situations in the world, as observers we are making a description that does not reflect the condition of structural coupling in which words are ontogenically established coordinations of behavior. Further, it also contradicts our understanding of the nervous system, since the nervous system does not operate with a representation of an independent world.

By contrast, instinctive communicative behaviors, whose stability depends on the genetic stability of the species and not on the cultural stability of the social system in which they take place, do not constitute linguistic domains: they do not give rise to ontogenically generated domains of coordinations of communicative behavior. The so-called "language" of bees, for instance, is not a language. It is a mixed case of instinctive and linguistic behaviors: there is a basically phylogenetic behavioral coordination here, but there are some group variations or "dialects" ontogenically determined.

It is apparent from this that the lack of similarity between a particular linguistic behavior and the action it coordinates (e.g., there is no similarity between the word "table" and what we do in distinguishing a table) is consistent with the underlying structural coupling. In fact, there may be any number of ways in which recurrent interactions that lead to coordination of behaviors are established between organisms (*table, mesa, Tafel*), in that what is relevant is the coordination of action they bring about, not the form they adopt. Indeed, linguistic domains arise as a cultural drift in a social system, with no preestablished design.

Linguistic Domain

Each time an observer describes the interactions that occur between two or more organisms as if the meaning he attributes to them determined the course of those interactions, the observer is making a description in semantic terms.

We call *linguistic* an ontogenic communicative behavior, i.e., a behavior that arises in an ontogenic structural coupling between organisms and that an observer can describe in semantic terms.

We call the *linguistic domain* of an organism the domain of all its linguistic behaviors. Linguistic domains are generally variable; they change along the ontogenies of the organisms that generate them.

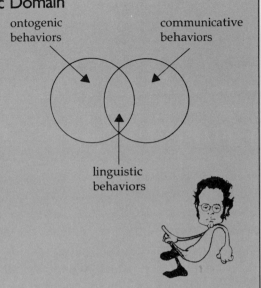

ontogenic behaviors

communicative behaviors

linguistic behaviors

The process is one of behavioral transformation contingent on conservation of the social system through the behavior of its components.

Human beings are not the only animals that generate linguistic domains in their social existence. What is peculiar to them is that, in their linguistic coordination of actions, they give rise to a new phenomenal domain, viz., the *domain of language*. This comes about through the co-ontogenic coordination of their actions. Essential to a linguistic domain is the co-ontogenic structural drift that occurs as the members of a social system live together. To an observer of the social system, from the outside it will appear as a remarkable congruence of a dance of coordinations. These coordinations of action bring forth different entities. In the flow of recurrent social interactions, language appears when the operations in a linguistic domain result in coordinations of actions about

> ## Language
>
> We operate in language when an observer sees that the objects of our linguistic distinctions are elements of our linguistic domain. Language is an ongoing process that only exists as languaging, not as isolated items of behavior.

actions that pertain to the linguistic domain *itself*. As language arises, objects also arise as linguistic distinctions of linguistic distinctions that obscure the actions they coordinate. Thus, the word "table" coordinates our actions with respect to the actions we perform when we manipulate a "table," obscuring the actions that (as operations of distinction) constitute a table by bringing it forth. In other words, we are in language or, better, we "language" only when through a reflexive action we make a linguistic distinction of a linguistic distinction. Therefore, to operate in language is to operate in a domain of congruent, co-ontogenic structural coupling.

It is not our purpose in this book to explore the many dimensions of human language. That is another book in itself. For our present purposes we wish to explore the key feature of language that radically modifies human behavioral domains and makes possible new phenomena such as reflection and consciousness. This key feature is that language enables those who operate in it to *describe themselves* and their circumstances through the linguistic distinction of linguistic distinctions. Such is our task in this chapter.

To an observer, linguistic coordinations of actions appear as distinctions, linguistic distinctions. They describe objects in the environment of those who operate in a linguistic domain. Thus, when an observer operates in a linguistic domain, he operates in a domain of descriptions. Moreover, language as a phenomenon takes place in the recursion of linguistic interactions—linguistic coordinations of linquistic coordinations of actions. Therefore, the linguistic domain becomes part of the environment in which linguistic coordinations of actions take place, and language appears to an observer as a domain of descriptions of descriptions. But what an observer does is precisely this: he makes linguistic distinctions of linguistic distinctions, or what another observer would say are ontogenically generated descriptions of descriptions. Hence, observing arises with language as a co-ontogeny in descriptions of descriptions. With language arises also the observer as a languaging entity; by operating in language with other observers, this entity generates the self and its circumstances as linguistic distinctions of its participation in a linguistic domain. In this way, meaning arises as a relationship of linguistic distinctions. And meaning becomes part of our domain of conservation of adaptation.

All this is what it is to be human. We make descriptions of the descriptions that we make (as this sentence is doing). Indeed, we are observers and exist in a semantic domain created by our operating in language where ontogenic adaptation is conserved.

In the case of insects, as we mentioned, cohesion of social unity is based on trophallaxis, the flow of chemicals between individuals, the exchange of chemicals between organisms. In humans, social unity is based on "linguallaxis" (a linguistic trophallaxis): a linguistic domain constituted as a domain of ontogenic coordinations of actions. We human beings are human beings only in language. Because we have language, there is no limit to what we can describe, imagine, and relate. It thus permeates our whole ontogeny as individuals: from walking to attitudes to politics. Before we examine further these consequences of language, let us see how it may have arisen and how it is a permanent biologic possibility in the natural drift of living beings.

For many years, it was a dogma of our culture that language is absolutely and exclusively a human privilege, far from the capacity of other animals. In recent years, this idea has been on the wane. This is due in part to many studies of animal life. These studies have shown that animals such as apes and dolphins display behavioral possibilities that we are not willing to grant them. Cogent evidence has come from studies with apes that show them capable of interacting with us in rich and even recursive linguistic domains.

Natural History of Human Languages

It is possible that from early times human beings have tried to teach apes (such as chimpanzees, which closely resemble human beings) how to speak. But it was only in the 1930s that scientific literature recorded a systematic attempt to do so. A pair of psychologists in the United States, the Kelloggs, brought up a baby chimpanzee together with their son. They intended to teach the animal how to speak. It was almost a total failure, for the animal could not reproduce the vocal modulations required to speak. Some years later, however, another couple in the United States, the Gardners, believed the problem was not in the animal's linguistic capacity: its abilities were not vocal but gestural, as is proverbial with monkeys. Thus, they decided to repeat the Kelloggs' experiment, this time adopting as a system of linguistic interactions only sign language, the comprehensive gestural language internationally used by deaf-mutes (Fig. 61).[11] Washoe, the Gardners' chimpanzee, showed that she was able not only to learn sign language (Ameslan) but to develop in it. So one might say that she learned how to "speak." The experiment began in 1966, when Washoe was one year old. By the time she was five, Washoe had learned a repertory of some two hundred gestures, including gestures functionally equivalent to nouns, verbs, and adjectives of the spoken language.

Now, the mere fact of learning how to make certain hand movements for the sake of a reward is not in itself a great achievement. Any circus animal trainer knows that. The question is: does

11. R. A. Gardner and B. T. Gardner, *Science* 165(1969):664.

Fig. 61. Sign language is not a phonetic but an ideographic language. Here, the gorilla Koko learns the gesture for "machine."

Washoe use these gestures in a way that convinces us that she uses them in language, just as human beings who converse in sign language use them? More than seventeen years later, after many hours of investigation, and many other chimpanzees and gorillas trained by different groups, the answer to that question is still fiercely debated by linguists and biologists.

Fig. 62. Interspecific linguistic interaction.

The answer, of course, depends on what counts as language. Some researchers have concentrated on the generative abilities of these animals to produce new concatenations of words; others have looked for grammarlike regularities. Thus, according to Lucy (another chimp trained like Washoe), a watermelon is a "fruit-drink" or a "sweet-drink," and a strong radish is a "food cry strong." And although she had learned a gesture for "refrigerator," Washoe preferred to signal "open drink eat." For us, the question of whether or not these (and many other similar) observations constitute evidence for language can be stated precisely. Can these primates interact with others in sign language as a linguistic domain, making linguistic distinctions of linguistic distinctions? Do they use Ameslan in recursive distinctions of actions they perform? Perhaps this is precisely what Lucy was doing when, on the verge of throwing a tantrum because she saw her human "parents" leave, she turned to her keepers and signed "Lucy cry." *Lucy* and *cry* are linguistic items in this example, and through them she engages others in a linguistic domain that all share, wherein there is linguistic distinction of an action performed. It seems to us that, at that point, Lucy is languaging.

The fact that primates can interact by using sign language does not necessarily mean they can use its potential richness to make all the linguistic distinctions that we human beings make. For instance, in a recent experiment, three chimpanzees trained in forms of linguistic interactions essentially equivalent to sign language were compared as to their ability to make generalizations.[12] The difference between one of them, Lana, and the other two, Sherman and Austin, is that in the latter there was an emphasis on the practical use of signs and objects in manipulating the world during their interactions with human beings and with each other. Lana, however, had learned a form of more stereotyped linguistic interactions: interactions through a computer. Stress was given to associating signs with objects. The experiment consisted in teaching the three animals to distinguish two types of objects: edible and nonedible (Fig. 63), which they separated on two different

12. E. S. Savage-Rumbaugh, D. M. Rumbaugh, S. T. Smith, and J. Lawson, *Science* 210(1981):922.

trays. Next, they were given a new series of objects and asked to place them on the corresponding trays. None of the animals had any problem in carrying out the task. After that, the animals were introduced to abstract visual images, or lexicograms, of edible and nonedible objects. They were

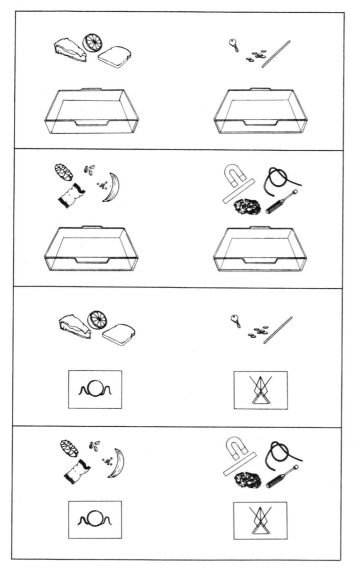

Fig. 63. Capacity for generalization according to different histories of linguistic learning.

asked to classify different objects according to these lexicograms. Lastly, the test was for them to associate the lexicograms with a new series of objects. In this experiment, Lana did poorly compared with her peers.

This experiment shows that Sherman and Austin could participate in generating the linguistic distinction of two operational categories, edible and nonedible (in what we as observers call a generalization); Lana could not. It seems that the greater ability manifested by Sherman and Austin in this experiment has to do with the rich versatility offered them by "interpersonal" interactions which Lana did not have.

All these studies on the linguistic capacity of higher primates—the chimpanzee, gorilla, and orangutan—help us understand the linguistic history of human beings. These animals belong to lineages that run parallel and very close to ours. Despite a 98 percent overlapping with humans in nucleic acid sequences, their behavioral preferences are very different from ours. This difference is, perhaps, the factor that restricts the expansion of the linguistic domains in which they participate. Thus, when these animals are submitted to a rich linguistic coupling—like Washoe—they are capable of entering into it, but the nature and extent of the linguistic domains in which they participate appear limited. This should not be surprising, however, since the differences between their evolutionary history and ours must have been a function of the conservation of different preferences in the modes of life.

We do not know the details of the evolutionary history of primate structural transformations that led to modern humans. Maybe we shall never know. Unfortunately, social and linguistic life does not leave obvious fossils. It is possible to make much of skeletal changes related to body posture and movement, manipulatory abilities, sound production, facial expression, and size and shape of the brain; however, it is not easy to reconstruct the details of modes of living conserved through evolution that resulted in the recursive expansion of our linguistic domains. What we *can* say is that the changes in the early hominids that made language possible relate to their history as social animals in close-knit interpersonal relationships, associated with collecting and sharing food. In that way of living, we see the coexistence and conservation of apparently contradictory activities, e.g., local interpersonal interactions in small groups of close-knit individuals that share food, having an outward independent mobility, without loss of emotional attachments, in the search for food or aesthetic space over fairly long periods. Such a way of living opens a realm of possibility for variations in the "trophallaxis" through which the group remains unified, as long as that way of living is conserved. Linguallaxis (linguistic trophallaxis) is highly suited for such variations. Unlike the chemical trophallaxis of social insects, it allows for limitless recursions in the coupling of behavioral capabilities of social individuals with the changes in social life that they generate, without the need for continual physical interactions. Let us examine this further.

The line of hominids to which we belong is a lineage more than 15 million years old (Fig. 64). But we cannot recognize in fossil remains prior to some 3.5 million years ago structural features characteristic of present-day humans, e.g., the skeletal features of full bipedalism, the increase in cranial capacity (Fig. 65), the opposing thumb in

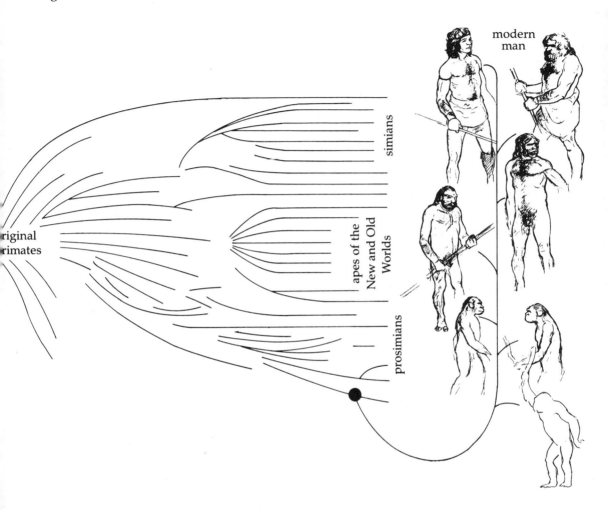

Fig. 64. Our lineage.

the hand, and a dental pattern related to omnivorous feeding habits based mainly on seeds and nuts. The same fossils reveal also that these early hominids lived in groups that included males, females, and children, who have been found together. Because of the anatomical features of their bipedalism, their sexual life must have engaged their linguistic interactions through facial expressions and frontal coitus. At the same time, females shifted from estral cycles to regular (nonseasonal)

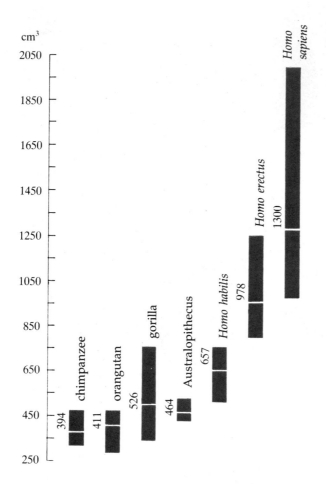

Fig. 65. Comparison of brain capacity in hominids

statistical average

sexuality—a strong factor in social bonding. We believe it is through the conservation of such styles of living, wherein linguistic interactions play a key role in the recurrent coordination of social actions, that language arose as a result of loving cooperation.

We can picture these early hominids as beings who lived in small groups, extended families in constant movement through the savanna (Fig. 66). They gathered food in the form of seeds and nuts, and occasionally they hunted. Since they walked

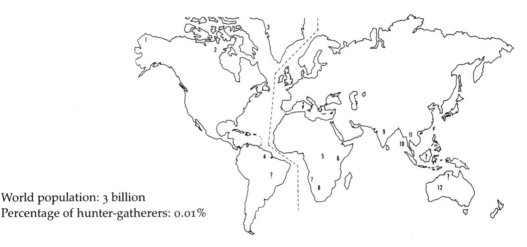

Worldwide Distribution of Hunter-Gatherers: 10,000 B.C.

World Population: 10 million
Percentage of hunter-gatherers: 100%

Known Locations of Contemporary Hunter-Gatherers

World population: 3 billion
Percentage of hunter-gatherers: 0.01%

Fig. 66. In the Neolithic period, human populations were
gatherer-hunters (*above*).
These origins are veiled in current life-styles (*below*).

1. Eskimos—Alaska
2. Eskimos—Northwest
   Territories
3. Eskimos—Greenland
4. Akuri—Surinam
5. Pygmies—Zaire
6. Ariangulos—Tanzania
   Boni—Tanzania
   Sanye—Tanzania
7. Korokas—Angola
   Bantus—Angola

8. Bushmen of Kalahari—
   South Africa
9. Birhar—Central India
10. Andaman Islanders—
    Andaman Islands
11. Rucs—Thailand
12. Aborigines—Australia
 ? Unverified presence of
   hunter-gatherers

on two feet, their hands were free to carry food back and forth among the members of their group; they did not have to do so in their digestive system, as in the case of other social animals that share food. This resulted in the integration of social life. Male and female were attached to each other by a permanent nonseasonal sexuality. Through conservation of food sharing and male participation in the care of the young, this led to a biology of cooperation and linguistic coordination of actions.

In other words, this way of life in ongoing cooperation and linguistic coordination of actions points to behaviors ideally suited for continual increase in the capacity to make distinctions within the realm of cooperative behavior up to our present biology of cooperative animals with linguistic reflection. This is hardly an accident. Indeed, this recurrent participation of hominids in the linguistic domains they generate through socialization must have been a determining dimension in any expansion of those domains, to the point of linguistic recursion that gives rise to language when linguistic behaviors become an object in linguistic behavioral coordination, in the same way as objects in the environment are tokens for recurrent linguistic coordinations. Thus, in the intimacy of recurrent individual interactions, which personalize the other individual with a linguistic distinction such as a name, the conditions may have been present for the appearance of a self as a distinction in a linguistic domain.

These are the main lines, as far as we can reconstruct, in the history of structural drift of hominids that led to the appearance of language. Further observations may change the details, but probably not the essentials since the fundamental biologic characteristics that made it possible are still with us, even if we have obscured them through competition and war.

Experimental Windows into Mental Life

Fig. 67. The Achilles' heel for oral human linguistic ability (in color).

The unique features of human social life and its intense linguistic coupling are manifest in that this life is capable of generating a new phenomenon, both close to and remote from our own experience: our mind, our consciousness. Can we pose some questions that will show this phenomenon in detail? Perhaps we could ask a primate: "How does it feel to be a monkey?" Unfortunately, we

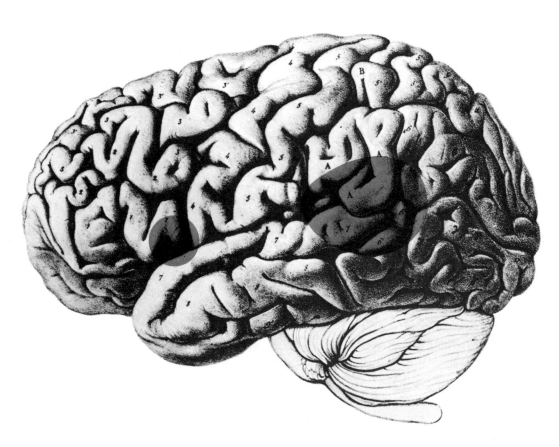

will never get an answer, for as soon as we build with them a realm of coexistence that admits such linguistic distinctions through language, monkeys will not be monkeys anymore; they will be unable to answer in terms of distinctions proper to them. The question, therefore, remains.

It could be that another way of contrasting human and nonhuman primate experience is not by language but by an object closely related to reflection—a mirror. Facing a mirror, animals generally behave either as if in the presence of another animal or with what we call indifference or avoidance. Thus, a dog may bark for a while in front of his image, then ignore it. A cat may show passing signs of fear and indifference. Among primates, a macaque will act much the same, displaying mostly aggression. A gorilla, however, when first confronted with a mirror will appear amazed and interested, but after becoming used to it, he will ignore it.[13] To explore further this reaction of the gorilla, experimenters anesthetized a gorilla. A colored dot was painted between his eyes—a place that could be seen only in a mirror. After awakening from the anesthesia, he was given a mirror. What a surprise! He put his hand to his forehead to touch the colored dot. Perhaps we expected the animal to stretch his hand and touch the dot in the mirror, where it could be seen. A macaque would not do what the gorilla did. Whatever the case with other animals, this experiment suggests that the gorilla can generate a domain of self through social distinctions. In that domain there is a possibility of reflection as with a mirror or with language. The mechanism for this may have arisen independently of either mirror or language. How this happened we do not know. But we presume it has to do with conditions similar to

13. G. Gallup, *American Scientist* 67(1979):417.

Fig. 68. Epileptic attack of an Inca king according to an engraving of the seventeenth century.

14. R. W. Sperry, *The Harvey Lectures* 62(1968):293.

those leading to the evolution of human linguistic domains.

A deeper understanding of the role played by linguistic coupling in generating mental phenomena in humans comes from observations made on patients under neurosurgical treatment for epilepsy. Epilepsy is a neurologic syndrome which, at its worst, produces centers that generate waves of electrical activity. These waves spread over the cortex without regulation (Fig. 68). Consequently, the person suffers convulsions and loss of consciousness, among a whole array of other disabling symptoms. In extreme cases of epilepsy, an attempt was made some years ago to avoid the spread of the epileptic fit from one cerebral hemisphere to the other. To that end, the corpus callosum was severed (Fig. 69).[14]As a result, the condition of the patients improved in terms of their epilepsy; however, their cerebral hemispheres stopped functioning as a unity. Because the corpus callosum has been cut, each hemisphere forms with the rest of the nervous system an operational unity in which the other cerebral hemisphere is left out as if it did not exist. It is as though after the operation the patient has become three different persons, each with its individual characteristics: a right-hemisphere person, a left-hemisphere person, and the external combination of the two in their operation through a common body. These three persons are not equally accessible to ordinary interactions, because all sensory systems have simultaneous access to both cerebral hemispheres; and we have to resort to special procedures to interact with one person independently of the other. For this reason, under normal conditions when we interact with one of these operated patients, we encounter the person that arises

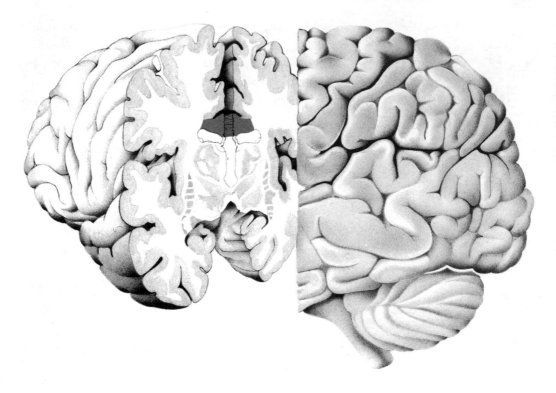

from the conjoined operations of the two hemispheres through a single body, and everything
seems normal.

What does 'all this reveal, and what happens
here with language and speech? We already mentioned that certain areas of the cerebral cortex
(called speech areas) have to be intact for speech
to be possible. Further, in most human beings it is
the speech areas of the left hemisphere that have
to be intact for a person to speak and understand
language. After the corpus callosum is cut, therefore, usually it is only the left-hemisphere person
who understands and generates language spoken
or written. How can we show this if the operated
patients are not readily distinguishable from ordinary people? To do this, we resort to some of the

Fig. 69. Interhemispheric dis-
connection in the treatment of
epilepsy: the sectioned corpus
callosum is shown in color.

anatomical features of the visual system that make it possible to interact independently with each of the disconnected hemispheres. Indeed, the connections of the retina to the brain are such that the entire visual field of both eyes to the left of a vertical line passing through a point of binocular fixation projects to the right hemisphere, and the entire visual field to the right of that line projects to the left hemisphere (see Fig. 70). Thus, when we ask a patient whose corpus callosum has been cut to fix his gaze at a point on a screen, we can interact visually with him through the right or left hemisphere, or simultaneously through both. It depends on where we project a test image on the screen with respect to the point of fixation.

Let us look at an example. An operated patient is asked to sit in front of a projection. While keeping his gaze on a fixation point, he must select from a set of objects hidden from view an object that corresponds to the image projected on the screen. If a spoon is projected on the left side of the fixation point (hence on the right hemisphere), the operated patient has no trouble picking up the spoon from the hidden set. If instead of a spoon we project on the screen to the left of the fixation point the word "spoon," the operated patient does not react at all. The word "spoon" does not exist for the right hemisphere person, with whom we have been interacting through the screen projections. Now, if the operated patient is asked what he saw when the word "spoon" was projected to the left of the fixation point, he admits to seeing nothing. Spoken and written language are usually as unintelligible for the right-hemisphere person, after the corpus callosum is cut, as for a baby or a monkey. The left-hemisphere person, however, after such an opera-

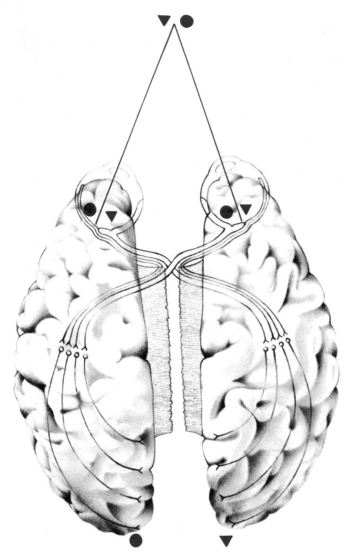

Fig. 70. Geometry of a projection of the retina to the brain. Perturbations located in the left side will exclusively affect the right side of the brain.

tion is usually able to understand written texts shown on the screen to the right of his fixation point.

· If we use this procedure and present a pinup girl to the right hemisphere of the operated patient, he will blush or show signs of embarrassment. But he will be unable to explain what happened. He may answer (as was the case): "Hey, doctor, that's quite a machine you've got there!" What happened is that, although the erotic image had been presented to the right hemisphere, the patient answered the question through the operation of his left hemisphere, which is the only one that can generate speech and which did not "see" the image. About all the left hemisphere can do is answer in a way that entails its connection with the rest of the nervous system and body; this is where the action of blushing or embarrassment generated through the right hemisphere took place. "That's quite a machine you've got there!" is how the operated patient lives through his left hemisphere the embarrassment generated through his right hemisphere.

Let us reflect further in this regard. There is a small percentage of people who can generate and understand language through the operation of both cerebral hemispheres. These persons do not show speech lateralization.[15] One of them was a fifteen-year-old patient named Paul from New York. After his corpus callosum had been severed, he volunteered for an experiment along the lines we described. Interestingly, he could participate in speech interactions through both hemispheres. One could ask each of them independently questions whose answers called for linguistic reflection. After the operation, Paul was able to select the spoon when asked to do so by the written word via either of his now independent cerebral hemispheres.

Consequently, a new experimental strategy was devised for Paul. The investigator would begin with a spoken question: "Who. . . ?" and the question was completed by an image projected on either side of the fixation point, for example, the

15. M. S. Gazzaniga and J. E. LeDoux, *The Integrated Mind* (Ithaca: Cornell University Press, 1978).

words ". . . . are you?" This question presented
to both sides got the same answer: "Paul." Likewise, to the question: "What day is tomorrow?"
both sides gave the same answer: "Sunday." Yet,
when the left hemisphere was asked, "What would
you like to be when you grow up?" the answer
was: "A racing car driver." This is fascinating, because the same question on the right side received
the answer: "A designer."

These observations show us that both the left-
and right-hemisphere persons in Paul are capable
of a behavior usually considered proper to a con-
scious mind capable of reflection. This is very
significant, because the difference between Paul
and patients who do not have the capacity to generate linguistic reflections independently with
both hemispheres shows that there is no self-
consciousness without language as a phenomenon of linguistic recursion. Self-consciousness,
awareness, mind—these are phenomena that take
place in language. Therefore, as such they take
place only in the social domain.

Paul's case points to something else. In all linguistic interactions with Paul, the left-hemisphere
person seemed to predominate. Thus, if a written
order such as "Smile!" was projected to the right
hemisphere, Paul did smile. Then, if the question
"Why are you smiling?" was presented to him
by his left hemisphere, the answer was "You're
funny." Likewise, if the order "Scratch!" was presented to the right hemisphere, Paul scratched.
But when the question presented to the left hemisphere was "Why are you scratching?" the spoken
answer was "Because it itches." The dominant-
left-hemisphere person, who had not seen the
order to scratch, had no trouble inventing a re-
sponse in line with his experience (scratching

himself) and reflecting how he lived that experience. What we say—unless we are lying—reflects what we live, not what happens from the perspective of an independent observer.

Mind and Consciousness

All these experiments tell us something fundamental about the organization and coherence in daily life of this ongoing flow of reflections that we call consciousness and that we associate with our identity. On the one hand, they show us that language is a condition *sine qua non* for the experience of what we call mind. On the other hand, they show us that our experiences flow according to coherences in the operation of our nervous system to which we have no access as observers but which necessarily occur as part of our ontogenic drift as living systems. No incoherence can occur in Paul's linguistic domain. Therefore, when asked for a reflection on something that arose in it, he must answer with an expression of that coherence: "You're funny" or "It itches." Identity and adaptation are conserved in his history.

In Paul's case, we see the operational intersection of three different persons in one body. At some time, these persons can be independent, self-conscious beings. This dramatically shows that it is in language that the self, the *I*, arises as the social singularity defined by the operational intersection in the human body of the recursive linguistic distinctions in which it is distinguished. This tells us that in the network of linguistic interactions in which we move, *we maintain an ongoing descriptive recursion which we call the "I." It enables us to conserve our linguistic operational coherence and our adaptation in the domain of language.*

Fig. 71. Experimental situation for the behavioral study of persons who have had a corpus callosum section. Positioned so that he can see neither his hands nor the objects to be handled, the subject is presented with images to the left or to the right of his visual field. He has to identify them with his hand or by speech.

This should not be surprising at this point in our presentation. Indeed, we saw that a living being exists only as long as it drifts in a domain of perturbations, regardless of the characteristics of that domain or how it changes because of its own operation. We then saw that the nervous system generates a behavioral dynamic through generating relationships of internal neuronal activity in its operational closure. The living system, at every level, is organized to generate internal regularities. The same occurs in the social coupling through language in the network of conversations which language generates and which, through their closure, constitute the unity of a particular human society. This new dimension of operational coherence of our languaging together is what we experience as consciousness and "our" mind and self.

Words, as we know, are tokens for linguistic co-ordination of actions and not things that we move from one place to another. It is our history of recurrent interactions that makes possible our ontogenic structural drift in a structural coupling that affords interpersonal coordination of actions; this takes place in a world we share because we have specified it together through our actions. This is so obvious that we are literally blind to it. Only when our structural coupling goes awry in some dimension of our existence do we realize (if we reflect on it) the extent to which our behavioral coordinations in the manipulation of our world and communication are inseparable from our experience. These breakdowns in some dimension in our structural coupling are common in our everyday life, from buying bread to bringing up a child. They are instances of change in the direction of our ontogenic structural drift in an infinite process of historical transformation. Indeed, we are usually unaware of the historical texture behind the linguistic and biologic coherences involved in the simplest of actions of our social life. Has the reader ever paid attention to the processes invariably entailed in the most trivial conversation: the generating of voice in language, the sequence in which words appear, the moment when speakers alternate, and so on? We usually do these things so effortlessly that everything in our daily life appears to us as simple and direct. In fact, our daily life appears to us so simple and direct that we often fail to see its richness and appreciate its beauty. Nonetheless, it is a refined choreography of behavioral coordination.

Thus it is that the appearance of language in humans and of the whole social context in which it appears generates this (as far as we know) new phenomenon of mind and self-consciousness as mankind's most intimate experience. Without an appropriate history of interactions it is impossible to enter into this human domain—recall the case of the wolf girl. At the same time, as a phenomenon of languaging in the network of social and linguistic coupling, the mind is not something that is within my brain. Consciousness and mind belong to the realm of social coupling. That is the locus of their dynamics. And as part of human social dynamics, mind and consciousness operate as selectors of the path which our ontogenic structural drift follows. Moreover, since we exist in language, the domains of discourse that we generate become part of our domain of existence and constitute part of the environment in which we conserve identity and adaptation. Robinson Crusoe knew this very well. That is why he kept a calendar, read the Bible every evening, and dressed for dinner. He behaved as if he were in England, living in the linguistic domain where he had his human identity and where he could conserve identity and adaptation. We who say these things as scientists are no different. Either we generate a linguistic domain (a social domain) through what we say and do, wherein our identity as scientists is conserved, or we disappear as such.

Every structure is compelling. We humans, as humans, exist in the network of structural couplings that we continually weave through the permanent linguistic trophallaxis of our behavior. Language was never invented by anyone only to take in an outside world. Therefore, it cannot be used as a tool to reveal that world. Rather, it is by languaging that the act of knowing, in the behavioral coordination which is language, brings forth a world. We work out our lives in a mutual linguistic coupling, not because language permits us to reveal ourselves but because we are constituted in language in a continuous becoming that we bring forth with others. We find ourselves in this co-ontogenic coupling, not as a preexisting reference nor in reference to an origin, but as an ongoing transformation in the becoming of the linguistic world that we build with other human beings.

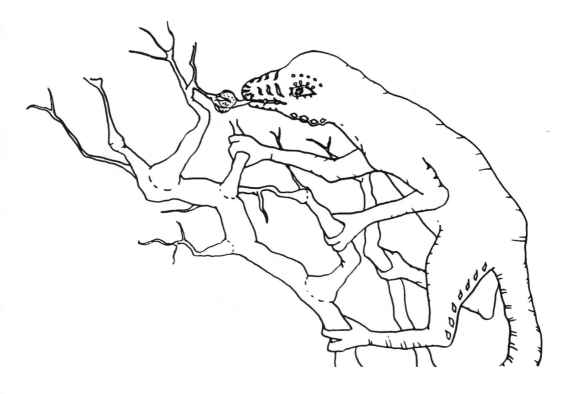

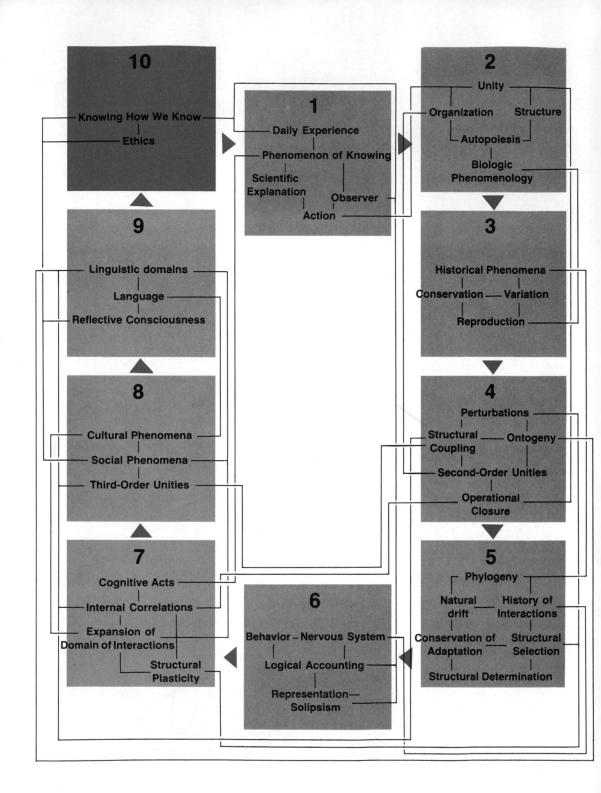

10 The Tree of Knowledge

Knowing and the Knower

Like the hands in Escher's engraving (Fig. 5), this book has followed a circular route. We began with the features of our experience common to our shared social life. From that starting point we moved on to cellular autopoiesis, the organization of metacellulars and their behavioral domains, the operational closure of the nervous system, the linguistic domains, and language. Along the way, we put together the building blocks of an explanatory system capable of showing how the phenomena proper to living beings arise. We came to see how social phenomena founded on a linguistic coupling give rise to language and how language, from our daily experience of cognition, enables us to explain its origin. The beginning is the end.

We have thus completed the task we set for ourselves, namely, that a theory of knowledge ought to show how knowing generates the explanation of knowing. This situation is very different from what we usually find, where the phenomenon of explaining and the phenomenon explained belong to different domains.

Now, if the reader has followed *seriously* what was said in these pages, he will be impelled to look at everything he does—smelling, seeing, building, preferring, rejecting, conversing—as a world brought forth in coexistence with other people

through the mechanisms we have described. If we
have lured our reader to see himself in the same
way as these phenomena, this book will have
achieved its first objective.

Doing that, of course, will put us in a circular
situation. It might leave us a bit dizzy, as though
following the hands drawn by Escher. This dizziness results from our not having a *fixed point of
reference* to which we can anchor our descriptions
in order to affirm and defend their validity. In
effect, if we presuppose the existence of an objective world, independent of us as observers and accessible to our knowledge through our nervous
system, we cannot understand how our nervous
system functions in its structural dynamics and
still produce a representation of this independent

world. But if we do *not* presuppose an objective world independent of us as observers, it seems we are accepting that everything is relative and anything is possible in the denial of all lawfulness. Thus we confront the problem of understanding how our experience—the praxis of our living—is coupled to a surrounding world which appears filled with regularities that are at every instant the result of our biological and social histories.

Again we must walk on the razor's edge, eschewing the extremes of representationalism (objectivism) and solipsism (idealism). Our purpose in this book has been to find a *via media:* to understand the regularity of the world we are experiencing at every moment, but without any point of reference independent of ourselves that would give certainty to our descriptions and cognitive assertions. Indeed, the whole mechanism of generating ourselves as describers and observers tells us that our world, as the world which we bring forth in our coexistence with others, will always have precisely that mixture of regularity and mutability, that combination of solidity and shifting sand, so typical of human experience when we look at it up close.

Nonetheless, we evidently cannot break away from this circle and step out of our cognitive domain. It would be like changing—by divine fiat—the nature of the brain, changing the nature of language, and changing the nature of our becoming. We would be changing the nature of our nature.

The fact remains that we are continuously immersed in this network of interactions, the results of which depend on history. Effective action leads to effective action: it is the cognitive circle that characterizes our becoming, as an expression of our manner of being autonomous living systems.

Through this ongoing recursiveness, every world brought forth necessarily hides its origins. We exist in the present; past and future are manners of being now. Biologically there is no way we can put in front of us what happened to us in obtaining the regularities we have grown accustomed to: from values or preferences to color qualities and smells. The biologic mechanism tells us that an operational stabilization in the dynamics of the organism does not embody the manner in which it originated. The business of living keeps no records concerning origins. All we can do is generate explanations, through language, that reveal the mechanism of bringing forth a world. By existing, we generate cognitive "blind spots" that can be cleared only through generating new blind spots in another domain. We do not see what we do not see, and what we do not see does not exist. Only when some interaction dislodges us—such as being suddenly relocated to a different cultural environment—and we reflect upon it, do we bring forth new constellations of relation that we explain by saying that we were not aware of them, or that we took them for granted.

That whole kit bag of regularities proper to the coupling of a social group is its biologic and cultural tradition. Tradition is not only a way to see and act, but also a way to conceal. Tradition consists of all those behaviors that in the history of a social system have become obvious, regular, and acceptable. Since they do not require reflection to be generated, they are invisible unless they fail. That is when reflection steps in.

All that we have in common as human beings is a biological tradition. It began with the origin of reproduction in autopoietic systems and a cultural tradition that started a few million years ago with the hominid lineage. This common biological heritage is the basis for the world that we human beings bring forth together through congruent distinctions. Despite those distinctions, nature is the same for all: we all agree that the sky is blue and the sun rises every day. At the same time this common biological heritage allows a divergence of cultural worlds brought forth through the con-

Fig. 72. *The Picture Gallery* by M. C. Escher.

stitutions of what can become widely different cultural traditions.

Thus, human cognition as effective action pertains to the biological domain, but it is always lived in a cultural tradition. The explanation of cognitive phenomena that we have presented in this book is based on the tradition of science and is valid insofar as it satisfies scientific criteria. It is singular within that tradition, however, in that it brings forth a basic conceptual change: cognition does not concern objects, for cognition is effective action; and as we know how we know, we bring forth ourselves. Knowing how we know does not consist of a linear explanation that begins with a solid starting point and develops to completion as everything becomes explained. Knowing how we know is rather like the boy in Escher's *Picture Gallery* (Fig. 72). The picture he looks at is gradually and imperceptibly transformed into . . . the city where the gallery and the boy are! We are unable to locate the starting point: Outside? Inside? The city? The boy's mind? Recognizing this cognitive circularity, however, does not constitute a problem for understanding the phenomenon of cognition. On the contrary, it constitutes the starting point that enables us to explain it scientifically.

The Knowledge of Knowledge Compels

When Adam and Eve ate the fruit of the tree of the knowledge of good and evil, says the Bible, they were transformed into different beings, never to return to their initial innocence. Before, their knowledge of the world was expressed in their nakedness. They went about with that nakedness in the innocence of mere knowing. Afterward, they knew that they were naked; they knew that they knew.

In this book we have harked back to the "tree of knowledge." We have invited the reader to eat the fruit of that tree by offering a scientific study of cognition as a biological phenomenon. If we have followed its line of reasoning and imbibed its consequences, we realize that they are inescapable. The *knowledge of knowledge compels*. It compels us to adopt an attitude of permanent vigilance against the temptation of certainty. It compels us to recognize that certainty is not a proof of truth. It compels us to realize that the world everyone sees is not *the* world but *a* world which we bring forth with others. It compels us to see that the world will be different only if we live differently. It compels us because, when we know that we know, we cannot deny (to ourselves or to others) that we know.

That is why everything we said in this book, through our knowledge of our knowledge, implies an ethics that we cannot evade, an ethics that has its reference point in the awareness of the biological and social structure of human beings, an ethics that springs from human reflection and puts human reflection right at the core as a constitutive social phenomenon. If we know that our world is necessarily the world we bring forth with others, every time we are in conflict with another human being *with whom we want to remain in co-existence*, we cannot affirm what for us is certain (an absolute truth) because that would negate the other person. If we want to coexist with the other person, we must see that *his certainty—however undesirable it may seem to us—is as legitimate and valid as our own* because, like our own, that certainty expresses his conservation of structural coupling in a domain of existence—however undesirable it may seem to us. Hence, the only possibility for coexistence is to opt for a broader perspective, a domain of existence in which both parties fit in the bringing forth of a common world. A conflict is always a mutual negation. It can never be solved in the domain where it takes place if the disputants are "certain." A conflict can go away only if we move to another domain where coexistence takes place. The knowledge of this knowledge constitutes the social imperative for a human-centered ethics.

What biology shows us is that the uniqueness of being human lies exclusively in a social structural coupling that occurs through languaging, generating (a) the regularities proper to the human social dynamics, for example, individual identity and self-consciousness, and (b) the recursive social human dynamics that entails a reflection enabling us to see that as human beings we have only the world which we create with others—whether we like them or not.

Biology also shows us that we can expand our cognitive domain. This arises through a novel experience brought forth through reasoning, through the encounter with a stranger, or, more directly, through the expression of a biological interpersonal congruence that lets us *see* the other person and open up for him room for existence beside us. This act is called *love*, or, if we prefer a milder expression, the acceptance of the other person beside us in our daily living. This is the biological foundation of social phenomena: without love, without acceptance of others living beside us, there is no social process and, therefore, no humanness. Anything that undermines the ac-

Ethics

Every human act takes place in language. Every act in language brings forth a world created with others in the act of coexistence which gives rise to what is human. Thus every human act has an ethical meaning because it is an act of constitution of the human world. This linkage of human to human is, in the final analysis, the groundwork of all ethics as a reflection on the legitimacy of the presence of others.

ceptance of others, from competency to the possession of truth and on to ideologic certainty, undermines the social process because it undermines the biologic process that generates it. Let us not deceive ourselves: we are not moralizing, we are not preaching love. We are only revealing the fact that, biologically, without love, without acceptance of others, there is no social phenomenon. If we still live together that way, we are living indifference and negation under a pretence of love.

To dismiss love as the biologic basis of social life, as also the ethical implications of love, would be to turn our back on a history as living beings that is more than 3.5 billion years old. We may resist the notion of love in a scientific reflection because we fear for the objectivity of our rational approach. Yet from what we have said in this book it should be apparent that such fear is unfounded. Love is a biological dynamic with deep roots. It is an emotion that defines in the organism a dynamic structural pattern, a stepping stone to interactions that may lead to the operational coherences of social life. *Every* emotion (fear, anger, sadness, etc.) is a biological dynamic which is deep-rooted and which defines structural patterns, stepping stones to interactions that may lead to different domains of operational coherences (fleeing, fighting, withdrawing, etc.).

Likewise, to disregard the identity between cognition and action, not to see that knowing is doing, and not to see that every human act takes place in languaging and, as such (as a social act), has ethical implications because it entails humanness, is not to see human beings as living entities. To do that—now that we know how we know— would bespeak self-deception. Whatever we do in every domain, whether concrete (walking) or abstract (philosophical reflection), involves us totally in the body, for it takes place through our structural dynamics and through our structural interactions. Everything we do is a structural dance in the choreography of coexistence. That is why everything we have said in this book is not only a source for scientific exploration but a source for understanding our humanness. We have delved into a social dynamics which points up a basic ontological feature of our human condition that is no longer a mere assumption, that is, *we have only the world that we bring forth with others, and only love helps us bring it forth*. If we have succeeded in bringing the reader around to this reflection, this book will have achieved its second purpose.

We affirm that at the core of all the troubles we face today is our very ignorance of knowing. It is not knowledge, but the knowledge of knowledge, that compels. It is not the knowledge that a bomb kills, but what we want to do with the bomb, that determines whether or not we use it. Ordinarily we ignore it or deny it, to sidestep responsibility for our daily actions, as our actions—all without exception—help bring forth and validate the world wherein we become what we become with others, in that process of bringing forth a world. Blind to the transparency of our actions, we confuse the image we want to project with the being we want to bring forth. This is a misunderstanding that only the knowledge of knowledge can correct.

We have reached the end. This book has invited you, the reader, to make a reflection. Such reflection will lead you to know your own knowledge. It is up to you to make this knowledge the pith and substance of your action.

A story is told of an island somewhere and its inhabitants.[16] The people longed to move to another land where they could have a healthier and better life. The problem was that the practical arts of swimming and sailing had never been developed—or may have been lost long before. For that reason, there were some people who simply refused to think of alternatives to life on the island, whereas others intended to seek a solution to their problems locally, without any thought of crossing the waters. From time to time, some islanders reinvented the arts of swimming and sailing. Also from time to time a student would come up to them, and the following exchange would take place:

"I want to swim to another land."

"For that you have to learn how to swim. Are you ready to learn?"

"Yes, but I want to take with me my ton of cabbages."

"What cabbages?"

"The food I'll need on the other side or wherever it is."

16. I. Shah, *The Sufis* (New York: Anchor Books, 1971), pp. 2–15.

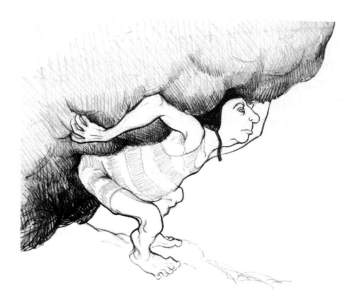

"But what if there's food on the other side?"

"I don't know what you mean. I'm not sure. I have to bring my cabbages with me."

"But you won't be able to swim with a ton of cabbages. It's too much weight."

"Then I can't learn how to swim. You call my cabbages weight. I call them my basic food."

"Suppose this were an allegory and, instead of talking about cabbages we talked about fixed ideas, presuppositions, or certainties?"

"Humm . . . I'm going to bring my cabbages to someone who understands my needs."

Glossary

amino acids:
: Organic molecules that are components of proteins. Each amino acid consists of an amine, an acid, and a molecular residue proper to each type of amino acid. There are some twenty different amino acids in the proteins of living beings, e.g., lysine, alanine, leucine.

anthropoids:
: Group of higher primates which includes gorillas, chimpanzees, gibbons, and orangutans.

axon:
: Protoplasmic neuronal extension capable of conducting nerve impulses, which issues (one per cell) from the cell body or a main dendrite of a nerve cell.

bacteria:
: Unicellular living beings that do not exhibit cytoplasmic compartmentalization (prokaryotes).

cell metabolism:
: The processes of molecular change that occur in the autopoiesis of a cell.

cerebellum:
: Part of the central nervous system of vertebrates that participates in the fine modulation of muscular activity generated through the operation of other parts of the nervous system.

cerebral hemispheres:
: The two anterior symmetrical brain portions of the central nervous system of vertebrates.

chromosomes:
: Nuclear dynamic macromolecular bodies made up of nucleic acids and proteins in nucleated cells. By extension, the nucleic acid ring present in bacteria. Chromosomes are easily seen during cellular division in nucleated cells and have distinct stable characteristics that are different for different species.

corpus callosum:
: System of axons that interconnects the cerebral cortexes of both cerebral hemispheres of mammals.

cortex:
: Superficial system of layers of neurons that cover the cerebral hemispheres.

dendrites:	Neuronal protoplasmic extensions that do not conduct nerve impulses. Neurons differ as to number, shape, and length of their dendrites.
DNA (deoxyribonucleic acid):	Principal nucleic acid component of chromosomes. It participates in the synthesis of cell proteins by specifying the amino acid sequence through the mediation of RNA.
estral cycle:	Periodic, seasonal, or monthly female sexuality in mammals.
eukaryotes:	Cells with cytoplasmic compartmentalizations such as nucleus, mitochondria, and chloroplast.
flagellum:	Cellular organelle shaped like a motile filament.
fossil:	Mineralized remains of a living system.
gametes:	Cells such as the ovum and sperm that fuse during sexual reproduction.
gene:	An operationally defined genetic unit that can be associated through protein synthesis with a segment of DNA.
hominids:	The group of primate species that includes modern *Homo sapiens* and its direct ancestors.
insulin:	A hormone secreted by the pancreas that participates in the organic regulation of the cellular absorption of glucose.
kiloparsec:	A unit of astronomic distance corresponding to approximately 3,260 light-years.
light-year:	A unit of astronomic distance corresponding to the distance that a beam of light would travel in a year. The speed of light is approximately 186,000 miles per second.
mitosis:	Process of cellular decompartmentalization leading to the reproduction of a cell.
myxomycetes:	A group of eukaryotic organisms whose life cycle takes place through several phases that include ameboid individuals and cellular aggregation with or without fusion.
neurons:	Cells that have an axon and a dendrite and that make up the nervous system as a network of interacting cells.
neurotransmitter:	Substance secreted at synaptic terminals which triggers electrical charges in the receptor neuron.
nucleic acid:	Chain of nucleotides. See *DNA* or *RNA*.
nucleotides:	Organic molecular components of nucleic acid. Each nucleotide is made up of a sugar molecule (ribose or

	deoxyribose), phosphoric acid, and a nitrogen base (purines or pyrimidines).
optic nerve:	Bundle of axons that issue from the retinal ganglion cells and end in different nuclei of the brain.
phenomenology:	The domain of all the phenomena defined in the interactions of a class of unities.
plasmodium:	Multinucleated unity resulting from the fusion of several unicellular eukaryotic individuals.
prokaryotes:	Cells without a nuclear compartment, e.g., bacteria.
proteins:	Organic macromolecules formed by the chains of many amino acids. These macromolecules fold in tridimensional shapes that have different characteristics depending on the sequence of amino acids that comprises them.
protozoa:	Free, living eukaryotic cells.
pseudopods:	Transitory protoplasmic expansions of ameboid cells.
recursive:	Referring to a process that operates on the product of its own operation.
rna (ribonucleic acid):	Nucleic acid that participates in the synthesis of proteins in the cell cytoplasm.
spores:	Cells that are covered by a resistant outer layer and participate as a dormant phase in the dissemination of many kinds of organisms.
synapsis:	The site of close contact between two neurons, usually between the axon of a neuron and the dendrites or the cell body of another neuron, but also between axon terminals or between dendrites.
thermonuclear reactions:	Transformation of elementary particles occurring under extremely high temperatures (on the order of 10,000°C).
trophallaxis:	Literally, from the Greek, "flow of foods," *trophallaxis* refers to the structural correlation that takes place between organisms through their interchange of food or secretions.
wavelength:	Length of the path traveled by a single wave cycle. The different colors of visible light and, in general, the different electromagnetic radiations are characterized by their different wavelengths.
zygote:	Cell resulting from the fusion of two gametes (sexual cells), the starting point in the development of a metacellular organism with sexual reproduction.

Sources of Illustrations

Fig. 1. *Christ Crowned with Thorns* by Hieronymus Bosch, National Museum of the Prado, Madrid.

Fig. 5. *Drawing Hands* by M. C. Escher, 1948 (28.5 × 34 cm), lithograph, reproduced from *The Graphic Work of M. C. Escher* (New York: Meredith Press, 1967).

Fig. 6. Photograph courtesy of Drs. L. Campusano and C. Monsalve, University of Chile. Photograph taken at Las Campanas Observatory, Chile.

Fig. 7. Taken from F. Hoyle, *Astronomy and Cosmogony* (San Francisco: Freeman, 1975), p. 276.

Fig. 9. Adapted from R. Dickerson and I. Geis, *The Structure and Action of Proteins,* (New York, Harper & Row, 1969).

Fig. 10. Taken from L. Margulis, *Symbiosis in Cell Evolution,* (San Francisco: Freeman, 1981), p. 117.

Fig. 12. Microphotograph of a leech embryo, courtesy of Dr. Juan Fernandez, Dept. of Biology, Faculty of Sciences, University of Chile, Santiago.

Fig. 14. Microscopy courtesy of Drs. Carlos Doggenweiler and Luis Izquierdo, Dept. of Biology, Faculty of Sciences, University of Chile, Santiago.

Fig. 19. *Water* by G. Arcimbaldo.

Fig. 20. Taken from J. T. Bonner, *The Evolution of Culture in Animals* (Princeton, N.J.: Princeton University Press, 1980), p. 79.

Fig. 21. Adapted from J. T. Bonner, *Scientific American,* 1959.

Fig. 22. Taken from J. T. Bonner, *Size and Cycle* (Princeton, N.J.: Princeton University Press, 1965), plates 6, 18, 25, 26.

Fig. 23. Adapted from J. T. Bonner, *Size and Cycle,* p. 17.

Fig. 24. Portrait of Charles Darwin, the Bettman Archives.

Fig. 26. Adapted from J. Valentine, *Scientific American,* September 1979, p. 140.

Fig. 27. Taken from S. Stanley, *Macroevolution* (San Francisco: Freeman, 1979), p. 68, according to the work of C. Teichert (1967).

Fig. 30. Adapted from R. Lewontin, *Scientific American,* September 1979, p. 212.

Fig. 31. Taken by Biruté Galdikos, in Brindamour, *National Geographic,* October 1975, p. 468.

Fig. 33. Photographs reproduced from C. Maclean, *The Wolf Children*, (New York: Penguin Books, 1977), figs. 14–16, 35.

Fig. 34. Adapted from F. Kahn, *El hombre*, vol. 2, p. 235, Ed. Losada, Buenos Aires, 1944.

Fig. 36. Taken from Santiago Ramón y Cajal, *Histologie du système nerveux*, vol. 1 (Madrid: Superior Council of Scientific Investigations, 1952), fig. 340.

Fig. 37. Adapted from J. T. Bonner, *The Evolution of Culture in Animals*, p. 61.

Fig. 38. Adapted from R. Buchsbaum, *Animals without Backbones* (Chicago: University of Chicago Press, 1948), fig. 14-1.

Fig. 39. Taken from J. T. Bonner, *The Evolution of Culture in Animals*, p. 59.

Fig. 40. Adapted from G. Horridge, *Interneurons* (San Francisco: Freeman, 1969), p. 36.

Fig. 42. Taken from R. Buchsbaum, fig. 84–1.

Fig. 43. Adapted from R. Buchsbaum, p. 73.

Fig. 45. Adapted from a serial reconstruction under electron microscopy by R. Poritsky, *J. Comp. Neurol.* 135:423, 1969.

Fig. 46. Taken from S. Kuffler and J. Nichols, *From Neuron to Brain* (Sunderland, Mass.: Sinauer Associates, 1976), p. 9.

Fig. 48. Adapted from D. Hubel, *Scientific American* 241:47, 1979.

Fig. 51. Adapted by N. Tinbergen, *Social Behavior of Animals* (London: Methuen, 1953), p. 10.

Fig. 52. Taken from E. Wilson, *Insect Societies* (Cambridge: Harvard University Press, 1971), fig. 801, according to an original by M. Wheeler (1910).

Fig. 53. Adapted from E. Wilson, fig. 14-9.

Fig. 54. Adapted from J. T. Bonner, *The Evolution of Culture in Animals*, p. 93.

Fig. 55. Adapted from E. Wilson, *Sociobiology* (Cambridge: Harvard University Press, 1978), fig. 25-3, according to an original by L. D. Mech (1970).

Fig. 56. Taken by I. DeVore and K. Hall, in *Primate Behavior* (New York: Holt, Rinehart and Winston, 1965), p. 70.

Fig. 57. Taken by V. Reynolds, *The Biology of Human Action* (San Francisco: Freeman, 1976), p. 53.

Fig. 58. Taken from J. T. Bonner, *The Evolution of Culture in Animals*, p. 121, according to an original sonogram by T. Hooker and B. Hooker (1969).

Fig. 59. Taken from J. Frisch, in *Primates* (New York: Holt, Rinehart and Winston, 1968), p. 250, according to an original photograph by M. Sato.

Fig. 60. Taken from C. Blakenmore, *The Mechanics of Mind*, Cambridge Univ. Press, 1978. p. 129.

Fig. 61. Taken from F. Patterson, in *National Geographic*, 154:441, 1978.

Fig. 62. Taken from C. Blakenmore, p. 125, from a photograph of the Institute for Primate Studies, University of Oklahoma.

Fig. 63. Adapted from E. Savage-Rumbaugh, D. Rumbaugh, S. Smith, and J. Lawson, *Science* 210:923, 1981.

Fig. 64. Adapted from J. Pfeiffer, *The Emergence of Man* (New York: Harper & Row, 1969), p. 8.

Fig. 65. Taken from V. Reynolds, p. 59.

Fig. 66. Taken from J. Pfeiffer, p. 311.

Fig. 67. Original drawing by Luis Gratiolet (1854) in his *Mémoires sur les plis cérébraux de l'homme et des primates*, plate I, fig. 1.

Fig. 68. Taken from C. Blakenmore, p. 158, according to the book by Guamán Poma de Ayala, *Nueva crónica y buen gobierno*, c. 1613.

Fig. 71. Adapted from M. Gazzaniga, *Scientific American* 217:27, 1967.

Fig. 72. The Picture Gallery, by M. C. Escher, 1956 (30 × 23.5 cm), lithograph, reproduced from *The Graphic Work of M. C. Escher*.

Index

Page numbers in *italics* refer to the Glossary.

Also in NEW SCIENCE LIBRARY

Awakening the Heart: East/West Approaches to Psychotherapy and the Healing Relationship, edited by John Welwood
Beyond Illness: Discovering the Experience of Health, by Larry Dossey, M.D.
Evolution: The Grand Synthesis, by Ervin Laszlo
Fisherman's Guide: A Systems Approach to Creativity and Organization, by Robert Campbell
The Holographic Paradigm and Other Paradoxes, edited by Ken Wilber
Imagery in Healing: Shamanism and Modern Medicine, by Jeanne Achterberg
The New Biology: Discovering the Wisdom in Nature, by Robert Augros and George Sanciu
No Boundary: Eastern and Western Approaches to Personal Growth, by Ken Wilber
Order Out of Chaos: Man's New Dialogue with Nature, by Ilya Prigogine and Isabelle Stengers, Foreword by Alvin Toffler
Perceiving Ordinary Magic: Science and Intuitive Wisdom, by Jeremy W. Hayward
Quantum Questions: Mystical Writings of the World's Great Physicists, edited by Ken Wilber
The Second Medical Revolution: From Biomedicine to Infomedicine, by Laurence Foss and Kenneth Rothenberg
Shifting Worlds, Changing Minds: Where the Sciences and Buddhism Meet, by Jeremy W. Hayward
A Sociable God: Toward a New Understanding of Religion, by Ken Wilber
Space, Time and Medicine, by Larry Dossey, M.D.
The Sphinx and the Rainbow: Brain, Mind and Future Vision, by David Loye
Staying Alive: The Psychology of Human Survival, by Roger Walsh, M.D.
The Tao of Physics: An Exploration of the Parallels between Modern Physics and Eastern Mysticism, second edition, revised and updated, by Fritjof Capra
Transformations of Consciousness: Conventional and Contemplative Perspectives on Development, by Ken Wilber, Jack Engler, and Daniel P. Brown
Up from Eden: A Transpersonal View of Human Evolution, by Ken Wilber
Waking Up: Overcoming the Obstacles to Human Potential, by Charles T. Tart
The Wonder of Being Human: Our Brain and Our Mind, by Sir John Eccles and Daniel N. Robinson